S0-ABD-728
hot Gimmick
KEEP OUT
KEEP OUT
KEEP OUT
KEEP OUT
KEEP OUT

Hot Gimmick

Volume 2
VIZBIG Edition

Story and Art Miki Aihara
English Adaptation Pookie Rolf
Touch-up Art & Lettering Rina Mapa
Original Shojo Series Design Judi Roubideaux & Izumi Evers
VIZBIG Edition Design Ronnie Casson
Original Shojo Series Editor Kit Fox
VIZBIG Edition Editor Yuki Murashige

Printed in China

Published by VIZ Media, LLC
P.O. Box 77010
San Francisco, CA 94107

10 9 8 7 6 5 4 3 2
First printing, June 2009
Second printing, October 2011

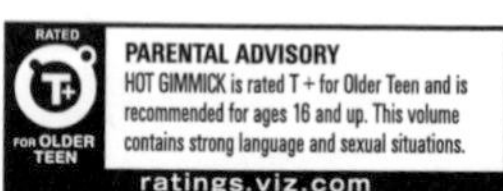

Hot Gimmick

Story & Art by
Miki Aihara

Shojo Beat Manga

VIZBIG Edition

Contents

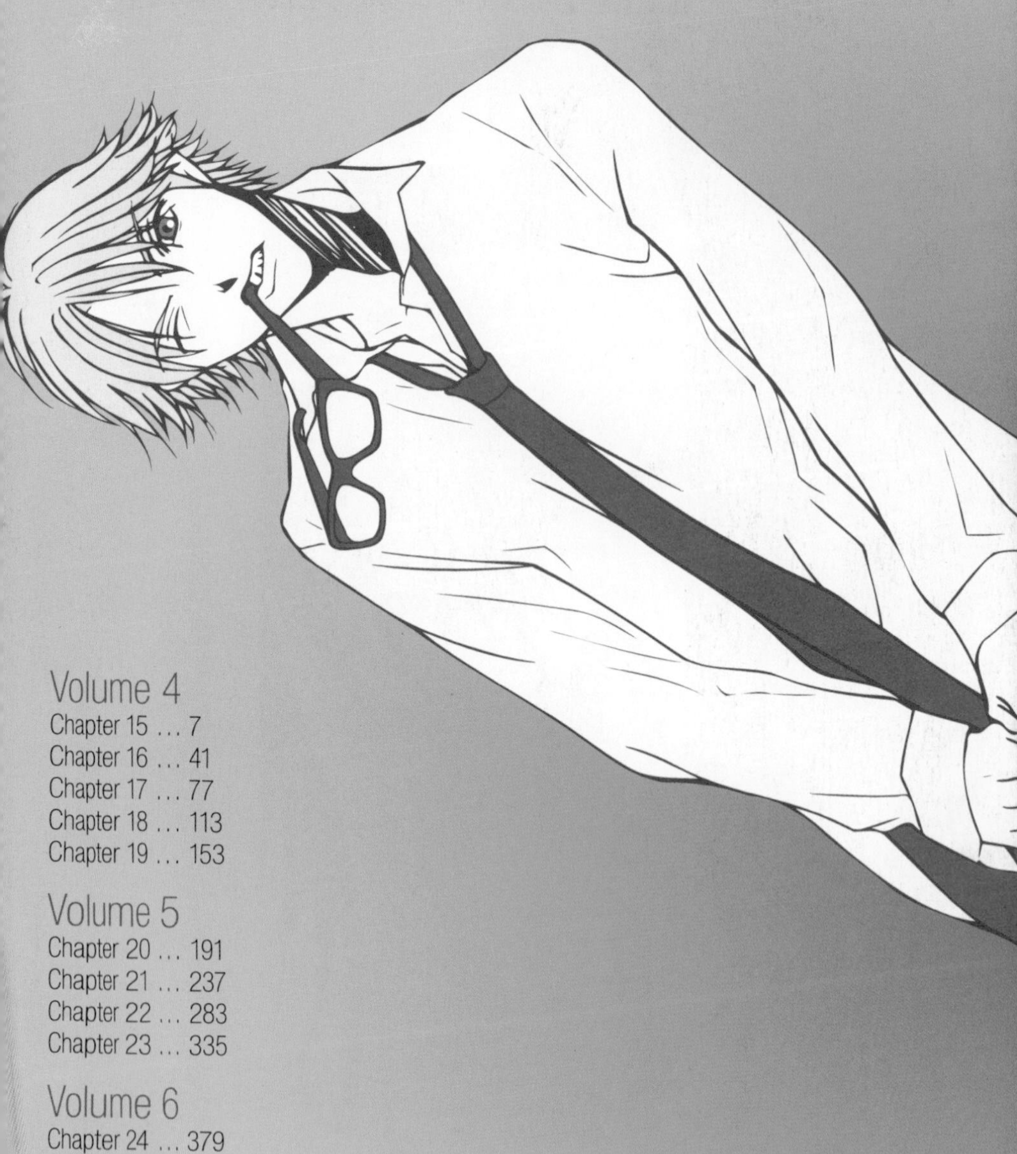

Hot Gimmick

vol.4

MIKI AIHARA

Chapter 15

...OH...

AZUSA...

SMILE

WHAT DO YOU THINK?

HOPE OUR SCHOOL'S OKAY ABOUT BLOND HAIR. IS IT?

I JUST GOT BACK FROM OKINAWA LIKE AN HOUR AGO.
THE PREZ TOLD ME TO STAY AWAY FROM HERE, BUT...
How ...?
ALL MY SCHOOL STUFF'S AT MY DAD'S, SO...
How can he...
AND I GOTTA MAKE UP FOR THE CLASSES I MISSED, STARTING TOMOR-ROW.
...talk to me ...
...like nothing happened ...?
RYOKI. DO IT WITH HATSUMI. RIGHT HERE. NOW.
I...
I...
...HATSUMI.
LOOK AT ME.
ULP

GO AHEAD, HIT ME. HARD AS YOU WANT.
...YOU DIDN'T SAY ANYTHING, DID YOU?
TO YOUR DAD. ABOUT WHAT I DID TO YOU.
HUH ...?
I WAS EXPECTING HIM TO COME STORMING OVER TO MY PLACE, SWINGING A HATCHET OR SOME-THING.
TSK! WHAT A LET-DOWN.
YOU WERE THAT CLOSE TO BEING GANG-BANGED AND EVERY-THING.

SMAK!
ULP
I'M SORRY...
I JUST...
COME ON, THAT WAS NOTHING.
PUT YOUR WEIGHT BEHIND IT. GIVE IT ALL YOU GOT.
I...
...CAN'T...
YOU'RE A MODEL. YOUR FACE IS...
PFFT!
THAT IS SO TYPICAL... JEEZ, HATSUMI.
AND I'M TAKING A BREAK FROM THAT, ANYWAY.
BUT I'M NOT APOLOGIZING.

I MOVED BACK HERE TO NAIL YOUR DAD.
TO WAIT AND WATCH FOR THE PERFECT OPPOR-TUNITY.
I'M HERE TO MAKE HIM SUFFER.
...SO I DON'T CARE...
...IF YOU HATE ME, HATSUMI. JUST GO AHEAD AND HATE ME.
AND I'LL DO THE SAME.
GOOD-NESS GRACIOUS! DID YOU SEE THAT?! JUST NOW!
THEY WERE KISSING!
I'M SURE OF IT!
THAT WAS THE OLDER NARITA GIRL, WITH THE ODAGIRI BOY...
OUT SO LATE, ALONE!
WHAT KIND OF MORALS DO HER PARENTS TEACH HER?!
I THINK WE OUGHT TO TELL MRS. TACHIBANA!

I wish I could... hate him.
Revolver
IS THAT YOU, HATSUMI?
...HEY! ARE YOU CRYING?!
OMIGOD! YOU OKAY?! WHAT HAPPENED?
OH... AKANE...

YOU CAME BACK... GOSH, I'M SO...
HUH?
OH. YEAH...
... GLAD... THANK GOD...
I'M SORR...
OH, AKANE! I'M SO SORRY ABOUT WHAT HAPPENED!!
GLOMP
BUT HEY, IT'S ALL OKAY NOW.
I TURNED HIM DOWN. I SAID NO. OKAY?!
SO DON'T SAY YOU HATE ME ANY-MORE...
OH... I'M NOT MAD AT YOU ANY-MORE.
IT WASN'T EVEN YOUR FAULT, ANY-WAY.
I WAS JUST TAKING IT OUT ON YOU, IS...
WAAH
...ALL.
WAITA-MINIT...
DID YOU JUST SAY YOU TURNED HIM DOWN?!
...Shh, Akane!
YOU IDIOT! WHADJA DO THAT FOR?!

I DON'T WANT TO BE HIS GIRL-FRIEND, OKAY?
OH! THAT REMINDS ME. YOU LIED TO MRS. T ABOUT ME AND RYOKI, DIDN'T YOU?
YOU HAVE NO IDEA, AKANE! ALL THE MEAN THINGS SHE SAID TO ME.
OOPS...
FOR-GOT ABOUT THAT.
SOR-REEE!
IT'S NOT A BIG DEAL, THOUGH, IS IT? YOU EXPLAINED, RIGHT?
IT'S OKEY-DOKEY?
AKANE! YOU SOUND PRETTY CHIRPY...
YOU AREN'T... UMM... UPSET ANYMORE? ABOUT RYOKI?
...MM-HMM...
I'M PRETTY MUCH OVER IT.
I CRIED IT OUT OF MY SYSTEM.
Oh, good.
She does seem to be feeling a lot better.
Wish it were that easy...
...for me, too.
But I have way too many problems right now...
YOUR PROBLEMS. WHAT ARE THEY?
SHARING YOUR PROBLEMS AND HELPING EACH OTHER OUT...
...MAKES YOU MY GIRL-FRIEND, RIGHT?

He just wants ...
...more material to black-mail me with. So he can push me around some more.
That's all it is.
There's no way he actually likes me for real.
Starting tomorrow, I bet...
...he'll be meaner to me than ever.
KISSING!
IN PUBLIC!
BEHAVING SHAMELESSLY! WITH THE ODAGIRI BOY!
RIGHT OUTSIDE THE ENTRANCE TO THE COMPLEX.
IN THE MIDDLE OF THE NIGHT!
IT WAS JUST DISGRACEFUL.
I CERTAINLY WOULDN'T LET MY DAUGHTER ACT LIKE THAT. WOULD YOU?
...WHAT'S THAT? YOU SAW HATSUMI-SAN...?
FIRST MY RYOKI, AND NOW THIS...
IT REALLY IS A BIT TOO MUCH.
I FIND IT QUITE OFFENSIVE!

THE PARENTS ARE EQUALLY TO BLAME, WOULDN'T YOU SAY?
I THINK THE NARITA FAMILY NEEDS TO BE TAUGHT A LESSON. THEY NEED TO LEARN THAT SUCH BEHAVIOR WILL NOT BE TOLERATED.
DON'T YOU AGREE?
YES, MRS. TACHIBANA!!
THUMP!
HI, HATSUMI! HOW ARE YA?
MORNING, SUBA...!!
HIYA, HATSUMI. AKANE-CHAN.
OH... UM, WE JUST BUMPED INTO EACH OTHER IN THE ELEVATOR.

OMI-GOD!
AZUSA-KUN! YOU'RE TOTALLY BLOND!
YOU LOOK SO GOOD LIKE THAT! ♡
THANKS.

WHERE'S RYOKI? DON'T YOU ALWAYS LEAVE TOGETHER?
UH, YEAH. I WENT OVER TO GET HIM, BUT HIS MOM SAID HE'D ALREADY LEFT...
OH...
...UM.
I'M IN A HURRY.

SO I'M GOING AHEAD.
WHAT?!
HANG ON, HATSUMI!
HAT-SUMI?!

JEEZ.
SHE DIDN'T HAVE TO RUN AWAY LIKE THAT.

I GUESS HATSUMI'S STILL PRETTY CUT UP OVER AZUSA.
MAYBE I OUGHT TO HELP HER OUT HERE. GET THEM BACK TOGETHER!

HEY, UM. HEY. UM.
IS SHE ALL RIGHT? IS SHE SICK OR SOME-THING?

GRRRRR
SNAP

I DUNNO. SHE PROBABLY GOT SICK WHEN SHE SAW YOU.
WHAAT?! COME ON!
WHY'M I PISSED OFF?

...

MATHEMATICS III
Matrixes and Curves
Popular edition
Buneido
BLAH
I DON'T LIKE BEING YOUR SLAVE...
BUT BEING YOUR GIRLFRIEND WOULD BE EVEN WORSE.

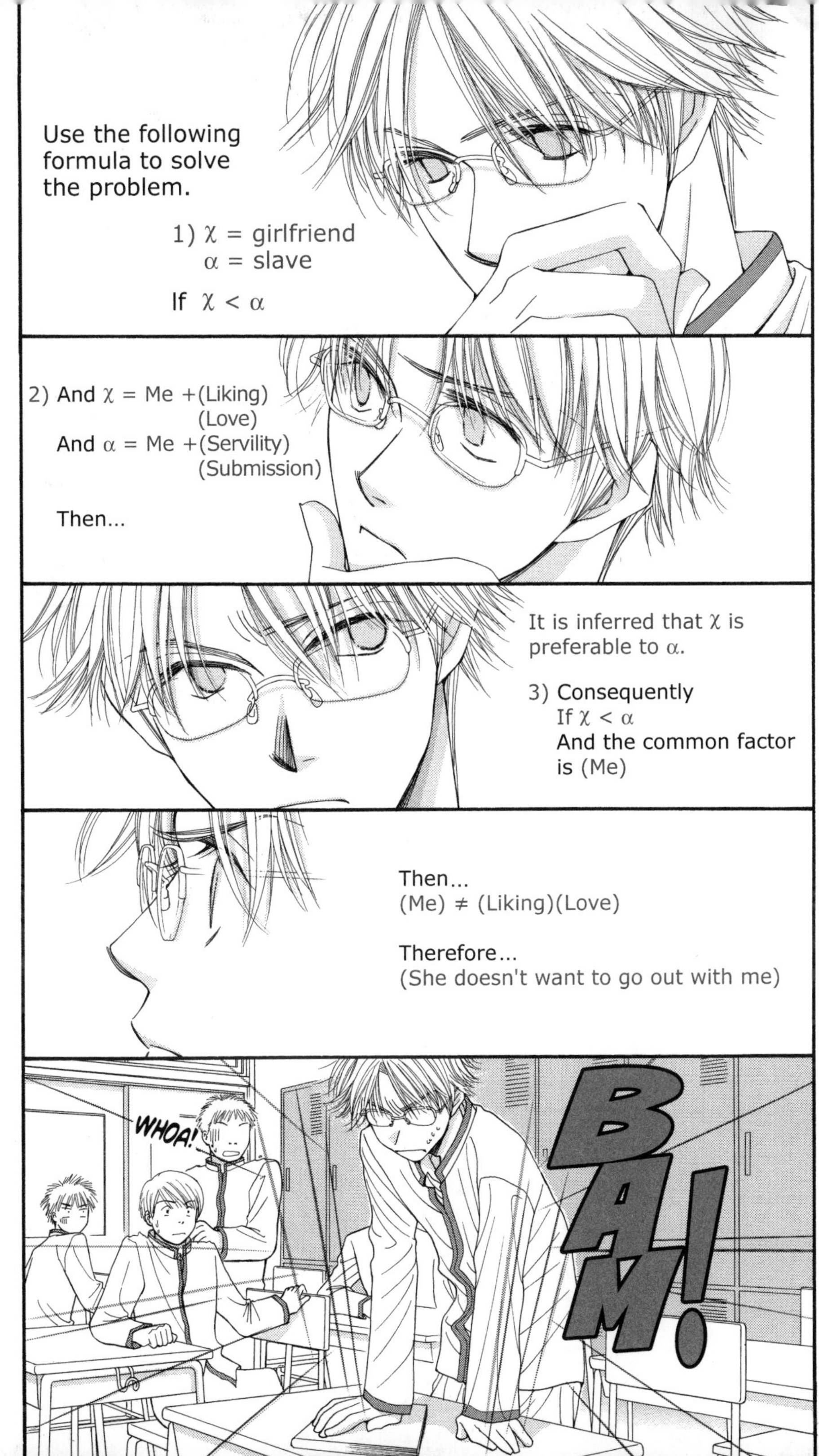

Use the following formula to solve the problem.
1) χ = girlfriend
α = slave
If χ < α
2) And χ = Me +(Liking)
(Love)
And α = Me +(Servility)
(Submission)
Then...
It is inferred that χ is preferable to α.
3) Consequently
If χ < α
And the common factor is (Me)
Then...
(Me) ≠ (Liking)(Love)
Therefore...
(She doesn't want to go out with me)
BAM!
WHOA!

...ER ...
WHAT'S UP, TACHI-BANA?
YOU SKIPPING LUNCH TODAY OR WHAT?
GRR GRR
FLASH
OH, DON'T TELL ME... YOU FOR-GOT YOUR LUNCH AT HOME?
WANT ME TO GO GET YOU SOME-THING?
HUH?
Revolve
1-2
DECEMBER 600yen
ACCESSORIZE!
165 Must-have items
By brand & by store
Special pull-out section
Original designer items
Work boots: a Compreher
Winter Fashion Q &
Tokyo/Paris
Man about tow
E STYLE OU WANT
Interview:
Cuff-Link
I CAN'T...
...HELP IT. I LOVE AZU --
THROB
LEMME SEE THAT.
GRAB
UH, SURE. BUT GIVE IT RIGHT BACK, OKAY?
IT JUST CAME OUT. I'VE HARDLY LOOKED AT IT YET.

RRRIIPPP!
WHOOPS!
HEEEY! MY MAAAG!
MY HANDS SLIPPED. BUT HEY, IT WAS AN UGLY COVER ANYWAY.
THE STYLE YOU WANT
INTERVIEW: CUFF-LINK MANIA
HOT FASHIO FOR YOU
KLAK
URGH URGH
WHY'S HE ALWAYS LIKE THIS?
PISSES ME OFF.
LIKE I COULD EAT LUNCH, ANYWAY.
I DON'T BE-LIEVE THIS.
...I'M SERIOUSLY PISSED OFF!
I'M GOING TO MAKE HER DO AS I SAY. NO MATTER WHAT!

TOK
TOK
TOK
TO
Azusa's still at school. He has those catch-up sessions.
Get home quick.
HUFF
HUFF
I don't want to see him.
OH, MRS. SUZUKI. MRS. DOI.
GOOD AFTERNOON!
...Uh, excuse me...?
OH ...
THAT'S ...
SHH !
Maybe they didn't hear me ...?
OH, HELLO. HOW ARE...
SHWA
HUH?!

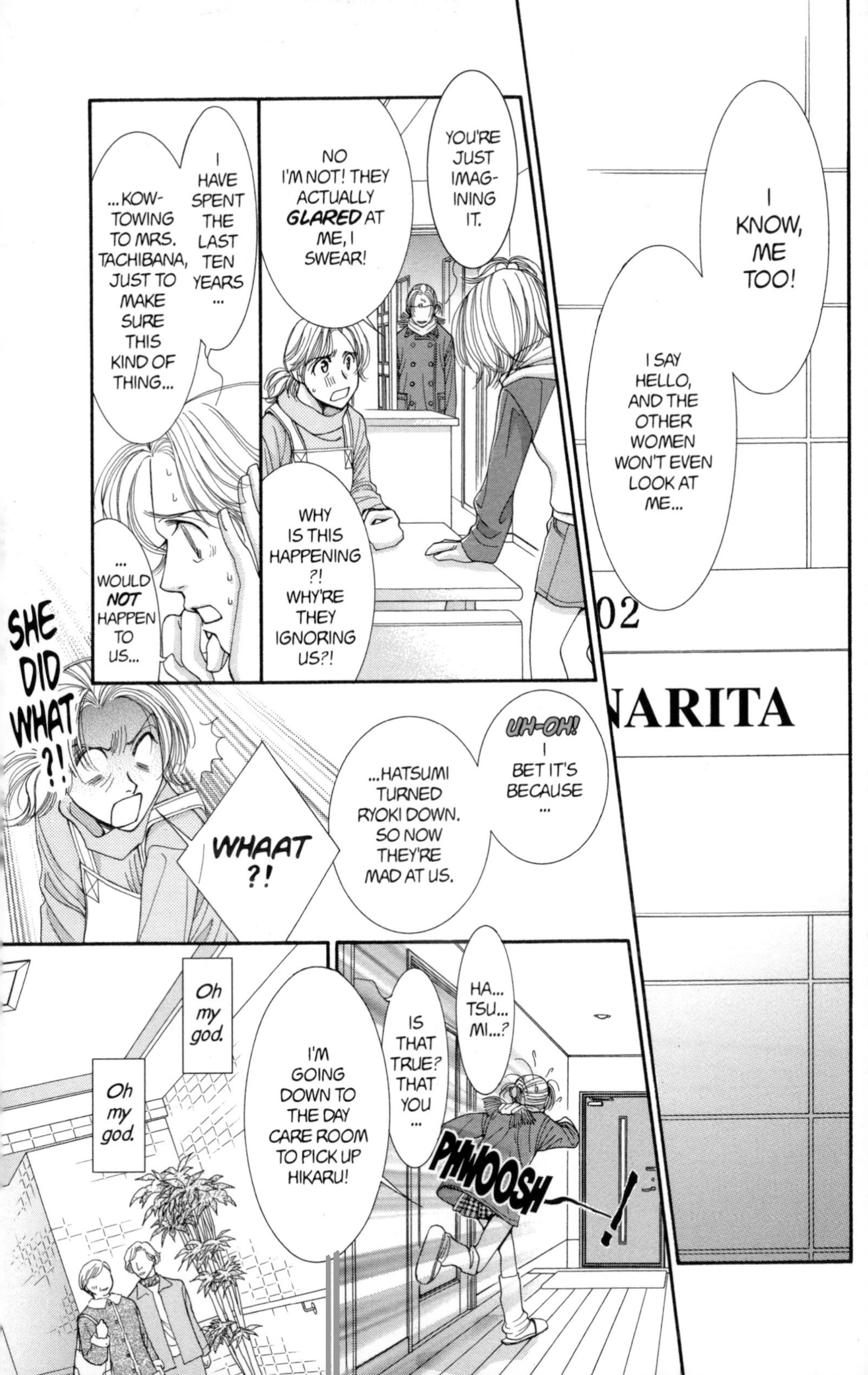
I KNOW, ME TOO!
I SAY HELLO, AND THE OTHER WOMEN WON'T EVEN LOOK AT ME...
02
NARITA
YOU'RE JUST IMAG-INING IT.
NO I'M NOT! THEY ACTUALLY GLARED AT ME, I SWEAR!
WHY IS THIS HAPPENING?! WHY'RE THEY IGNORING US?!
I HAVE SPENT THE LAST TEN YEARS...
...KOW-TOWING TO MRS. TACHIBANA, JUST TO MAKE SURE THIS KIND OF THING...
...WOULD NOT HAPPEN TO US...
UH-OH! I BET IT'S BECAUSE...
...HATSUMI TURNED RYOKI DOWN. SO NOW THEY'RE MAD AT US.
WHAAT?!
SHE DID WHAT?!
HA... TSU... MI...?
IS THAT TRUE? THAT YOU...
I'M GOING DOWN TO THE DAY CARE ROOM TO PICK UP HIKARU!
PHWOOSH—!
Oh my god.
Oh my god.

Is that...
Is that really why?!
GOOD...
AFTER-NOO--
HOO HOO
EXACT-LY! SO I...
... TRIED THE RECIPE MYSELF, AND...
YOU DID? IT SEEMS SO COMPLI-CATED!
HOW'D IT TURN OUT?
HOO HOO
DAY CARE ROOM
KREE

KREE KREE
UMM...
I'M HERE TO PICK UP HIKARU NARITA...
OH... YES...
COME IN...
TOK TOK TOK TOK TOK
BWOMF
HIKARU?
HAMI-CHAN, I WANNA GO HOME.
NOBODY'S PLAYING WITH ME TODAY.
THEY CAN'T PLAY WITH ME, THEY SAID.
WHAT?!
BUT...
THAT'S SO...
BYE-BYE!
OKAY, EVERY-BODY. LET'S CLEAN UP!

LET'S BE REAL GOOD UNTIL YOUR MOMMIES GET HERE, OKAY?
OKAAY!
So easily?
Is this... possible?
Is it really?
So soon...?
I can't believe it.
MOVE IT!
WHUMP
HIKARU!

ARE YOU OKAY?! HIKARU?
THUD
HA HA HA HA
KWIP
WELL, THEY *WERE* BLOCKING THE PATH, WEREN'T THEY?
SO INCONSIDERATE!
COME HERE, YOU TWO.
LET'S GO. WE'LL GET IN TROUBLE IF MRS. TACHIBANA SEES US TALKING TO HER!
HIC
HIC

So it was ...
... Mrs. Tachibana, after all.
...'ERE YOU GO.
YOU OKAY? NOTHING HURTS?
ULP
JEEZ...
POOR KID. I DON'T BELIEVE THIS.

PROUD OF YOUR-SELVES?
AZU...
BUNCHA GROWN-UPS GANGING UP ON A LITTLE KID?
AGH!
Smak!
AAAAH! MY DARLING!
mom
HEY! WHAT'RE YOU DOING?!
THAT'S FOR WHAT HE DID TO HIKARU. I SAY THAT MAKES US EVEN.
OR YOU WANT TO DIS ME, TOO?

ARE YOU AL RIGH ?!
WAAAAH! IT HURTS!
COME ON, HATSUMI.
LET'S JUST GO.
DA-DOOM
DA-DOOM
DA-DOOM
DA-DOOM
Don't be glad. Don't even think about it.
And stop feeling so nervous and excited.

LET GO... OF MY HAND...
HUH?
OH! RIGHT. SORRY.
ARE YOU... BEING NICE... SO YOU CAN...
...DUPE ME... AGAIN...?
...HA-TSUMI...
IS THIS... ANOTHER TRICK?

HFF
I'M NOT...
...BEING NICE TO **YOU**, HATSUMI. IT'S JUST...
I HATE THAT KIND OF THING, THAT'S ALL.
I WAS ONLY HELPING HIKARU.
OH...!
HIKARU! I'M SO SORRY!!
It's all my fault.
This is all because I turned him down.
HUG
OUCH, HAMI-CHAN. THAT HUR--
HEY, IT'S RYOKI!

YO!
HOW'S IT GOIN', RYOKI?

AZUSA ...
YOU...!

I THOUGHT I TOLD YOU TO STAY AWAY FROM HERE!
UMM!
RYOKI?!
AHM... I... UH...
I'D, UM, LIKE TO... TALK TO YOU...
UH... YEAH? UH... HUH.
AZUSA? COULD YOU TAKE HIKARU UP TO MY HOUSE FOR ME?
HEY!
YOU'RE ASKING **HIM** TO LOOK AFTER YOUR BROTHER?!
SHWA
...**HEY.**
YOU **CRAZY** OR SOME-THING?!
WHY'RE YOU EVEN **TALKING** TO THAT BASTARD AFTER WHAT HE DID TO YOU?!

JEEZ, LIKE HE'S YOUR FRIEND OR SOME-THING.
...I'M... SORRY...
ABOUT... YESTER-DAY...
UH... MHM?!
PLEASE... I APOLO-GIZE. I'M REALLY SORRY.
PLEASE STOP MAKING EVERYONE HERE IGNORE US...
HUH?! WHAT'RE YOU TALKING ABOUT ...?
PLEASE!
I DON'T CARE IF IT'S JUST ME, BUT...
I'M SORRY I MADE YOU ANGRY.
HANG ON A SEC! I DON'T KNOW WHAT THE HELL YOU --
I have to do this...
...for Hikaru.
And Shinogu and Akane.
And for Mom. ...And Dad.
I'LL BE YOUR SLAVE AND EVERY-THING.

I... I APOLOGIZE... FOR WHAT I SAID...
I'LL OBEY YOU FROM NOW ON...
I'LL DO... WHATEVER YOU SAY...
...THIS ISN'T...
...WHAT I MEANT ...AT ALL...
YOU JUST DON'T GET IT.
...GIMME A BREAK...
HUH ...?!

WAIT...! RYOKI...
...THAT...
IS NOT WHAT I WANT, ALL RIGHT?
SHOO
What do I do now?
How ...
...did it end up like this?

WAAH. WHAT CAN I DO...?

Chapter 16

BUT I DIDN'T DO ANYTHING!

About a week since my family became...

...the local outcasts...

GOOD MORNING!

OH, GOOD MORNING!

MORNING!

THEY'RE ONLY PICKING UP RECYCLABLE GARBAGE TODAY.

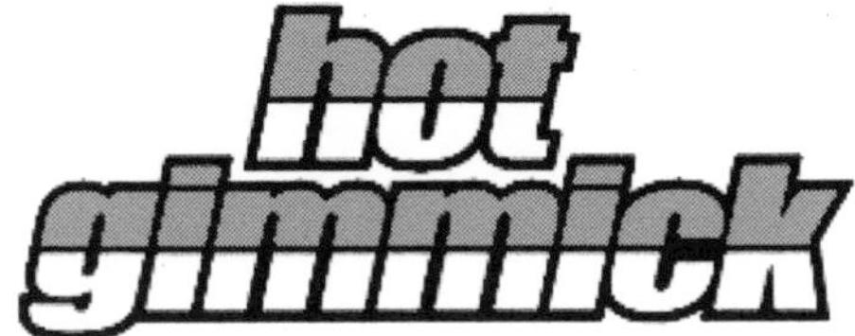

GOOD...
GOOD MORNING, EVERY-BODY!
...MORN-ING!
GOOD MORNING, MRS. TACHIBANA!
THIS IS OUR ...
IF YOU COULD ...
PFUI!
CANS OVER THERE! THIS IS GLASS.
JUST HURRY UP AND PUT IT DOWN.
RUSH
UH, UMM! MRS. TACHI-BANA?
I...
KRASH!
OH NO...
HEY! WHAT'RE YOU DOING? WE JUST SORTED THAT.
KLANK KLANK KLANK
I'M SO SORRY ...
THIS IS A LOT OF WORK HERE, YOU KNOW?
NOW LOOK WHAT YOU DID!

OH DEAR! ARE YOU ALL RIGHT, MRS. TACHIBANA? DID YOU GET SPLASHED OR ANY-THING?
I'M FINE.
PICK UP THE MESS YOU MADE!
REALLY! HOW CLUMSY CAN YOU GET?
HISS
HISS
HISS
DON'T HELP THEM. WE'LL GET IN TROUBLE IF WE DO.
YOU SEE HOW MRS. HONDA'S GROUP TREATS THEM?
WELL, THEY'RE BASICALLY MRS. TACHIBANA'S PRESIDENTIAL GUARD, SO --
HATSUMI ...
YIPES
YOU KNOW WHAT AKANE SAID? WAS THAT TRUE?
DID YOU REALLY... REFUSE... RYOKI?
...
...UH ...
UMM ...
I DIDN'T REALLY REFUSE HIM SO MUCH AS... UMM...
WELL, I PISSED HIM OFF, SORTA...UH... YOU COULD SAY WE GOT IN A FIGHT, SORTA...
...HA-TSUMI.
I DON'T LIKE TO IN-TERFERE IN YOUR FRIEND-SHIPS, BUT...
I WISH YOU COULD'VE AVOIDED UPSETTING THE TACHIBANAS, YOU KNOW...?
I'M...
... SORRY ...
WELL, IT'S TOO LATE NOW. GO AHEAD TO SCHOOL. I'LL DO THE REST.

PLOD
PLOD
OH... UH...
GOOD MORN-ING.
SIGH
SO HELP HER OUT.

AZUSA ...
HIYA.
LOOK, YOU'RE THE ONLY ONE WHO *CAN* HELP HER OUT.
YOUR MOM'S THE RINGLEADER, AFTER ALL.
PLEASE STOP MAKING EVERYONE HERE IGNORE US.
I'LL DO WHATEVER YOU SAY.
...IT'S NONE OF YOUR BUSI-NESS.
HELP HER OUT, AND SHE MIGHT WANNA BE YOUR GIRLFRIEND. YOU KNOW...
...WHEN SHE REALIZES THERE'RE SOME PERKS.

...YOU REALLY ...
PISS ME OFF, YOU KNOW THAT?
AND HERE I'M JUST TRYING TO GIVE YOU A LITTLE ADVICE.
IF YOU WASTE TOO MUCH TIME, SOMEBODY ELSE IS GONNA GET HER. SEE? OVER THERE.
HUH?!
Wanna walk together?
Oh! Shinogu...
...JEEZ! IT'S HER GODDAMN BROTHER, FER CHRISSAKE ...
WELL, THOSE TWO ARE REAL CLOSE. I MEAN REAL CLOSE.
...YOU SOUND LIKE YOU'RE TRYING TO INSINUATE SOMETHING.
WHAT EXACTLY DO YOU --
RYOKI DEAR!
OH GOOD, I WAS ABLE TO CATCH YOU. THERE WAS SOMETHING I FORGOT TO MENTION.
OH, WERE YOU TALKING TO AZUSA-SAN?
GOOD MORNING!

YOU'RE AS BEAUTIFUL AS ALWAYS, MRS. TACHIBANA.
SEE YOU, RYO. I'LL GO ON AHEAD.
OH MY! SUCH A LITTLE CHARMER, THAT BOY!
TCH!
BUT HE REALLY IS QUITE NAÏVE, ISN'T HE?
MAYBE THAT'S WHY HE FELL INTO THE CLUTCHES OF THAT HATSUMI-SAN, POOR BOY.
WHAT?!
WHAT DO YOU MEAN BY THAT, MOTHER?
WELL, SOMEONE SAW THAT AWFUL GIRL...
...EMBRACING AZUSA-SAN IN FRONT OF THE GATE TO THE COMPLEX. SIMPLY SHAMEFUL! OR SHOULD I SAY, SHAME*LESS*!
OUR NEIGHBORS FIND IT QUITE OBJECTIONABLE, AND THEY'VE BEEN AVOIDING THE NARITA FAMILY EVER SINCE.
I REALLY THINK YOU OUGHT TO AVOID THAT HATSUMI-SAN YOURSELF.
BUT OH! BEFORE I FORGET. THIS IS FAR MORE IMPORTANT. YOUR NEW TUTOR WILL BE COMING OVER THIS EVENING.
SO PLEASE BE HOME BY SEVEN O'CLOCK, ALL RIGHT?

...I'M SORRY, SHINOGU...YOU'RE BEING IGNORED BY EVERYBODY TOO, AREN'T YOU? I'M REALLY SORRY.
I HAD NO IDEA IT WOULD TURN INTO SOMETHING LIKE THIS...
I DIDN'T REALIZE...
THAT... MAKING RYOKI ANGRY WOULD LEAD TO... *THIS*...
HEY, IT REALLY DOESN'T BOTHER ME.
AND IT ISN'T YOUR FAULT. DON'T WORRY ABOUT IT.
...BUT IT'S REALLY GETTING TO MOM. AND HIKARU...
...DOESN'T WANT TO GO DOWN TO THE DAY CARE ROOM ANYMORE.
...THAT SUCKS. POOR LITTLE GUY. THOSE ASSHOLES!
SO WHAT HAPPENED, ANYWAY? HOW'D YOU PISS HIM OFF?
YIPES

...DON'T TELL MOM ABOUT THIS, OKAY?
BUT... FOR SOME REA-SON, HE...
HE ...
... SUDDENLY WANTED ME TO BE HIS GIRL-FRIEND...
JOLT
AND I SAID NO, AND THEN...
SO WHAT'S WRONG WITH THAT?!
UH ...
NOTHING, OF COURSE...
YOU BET THERE'S NOTHING WRONG WITH IT!
THAT GODDAMN PUNK!
THIS IS RIDICULOUS! I'M TELLING MRS. T EXACTLY WHAT I THINK OF HER AND HER SON AND ALL HER CRONIES!
NO! SHINOGU, PLEASE!
WE CAN'T PISS THEM OFF ANY FURTHER!
I'LL GO AND APOLO-GIZE AGAIN.
WHAAT ?!
THIS IS SO HARD ON MOM AND ON HIKARU.
IT'S REALLY TOUGH FOR THEM.

IF THAT'S ALL IT TAKES TO GET THINGS BACK THE WAY THEY WERE...
I'LL APOLOGIZE. IF THAT'LL MAKE THINGS NORMAL AGAIN, IT'S WORTH IT.
I'LL APOLOGIZE. I'LL DO ANYTHING IT TAKES.
I'LL AGREE TO BE HIS SLAVE EVEN!
HA...TSUMI...
I JUST WANT IT TO BE LIKE BEFORE...
SKWEEZ
...ALL RIGHT.
I'LL GO WITH YOU.
WHY SHOULD YOU DO THE HARD STUFF ALL BY YOUR-SELF?

...WELL, AGREEING TO BE HIS SLAVE IS GOING A BIT TOO FAR.
HA HA HA HA
YOU KIDDING ME? IF HE EVEN ***THOUGHT*** IT, I'D PERSONALLY WRING HIS GODDAMN NECK. (FOR REAL.)
UNGH!
WELL... ACTUALLY HE MADE ME HIS SLAVE WAY BACK...AND FORCED ME TO DO ALL KINDS OF STUFF...
PAT PAT

He told me to wait until he gets off work...
But I probably ought to go by myself.
There's so much stuff that would send Shinogu through the roof if he found out...
SIGH...
soul
I wish...
...I didn't have to do this...

HEY, HATSUMI-- WANNA GO HOME TOGETHER?
UH...
YEAH. SURE.
What am I doing?
HIGASHI KOMAZAWA STATION
What am I hoping for?
I really am stupid.
Azusa hates me.
What is wrong with me?

SIGH
YOU'RE LATE.
HOW MANY HOURS DID YOU EXPECT ME TO WAIT HERE?
YOU DON'T EVEN HAVE ANY AFTER-SCHOOL STUFF, FER CHRISSAKE!
Actually waited only 30 minutes.
HEY...

THAT WAS RYOKI AND HATSUMI ...
OMI-GOD!
HEY! SUBARU! DIDJA SEE THAT?

THAT WAS HATSUMI WITH RYOKI, WASN'T IT?!
WAA!
UH...
SHOULD WE LET HER GO OFF WITH HIM LIKE THAT?!
HE'S TOTALLY PISSED OFF AT HER, RIGHT?!

HUH ...?
OH, COME ON!
YOU KNOW MY WHOLE FAMILY'S BEING DISSED BY EVERYONE IN THE COMPLEX!

REMEMBER HATSUMI SAID SHE TURNED RYOKI DOWN?
WELL, IT STARTED THE VERY NEXT DAY...

GOTTA SAY, IT'S KIND OF A LETDOWN... HERE I THOUGHT HE WAS SO GREAT...
AND THEN HE GOES CRYING TO HIS MOM AND MAKES HER PUNISH US.
YOU'RE WRONG.
RYO WOULD NEVER DO SOME-THING LIKE THAT.
THERE'S JUST NO WAY.

SURE HE'S ARROGANT, AND KINDA STUCK-UP ABOUT HIS FAMILY AND ALL...
BUT HE DOESN'T TELL ON PEOPLE OR GANG UP ON THEM EITHER.
SO... I'M PRETTY SURE HE HAS NOTHING TO DO WITH THIS.
RYOKI! LET GO OF MY HAND.
WHAT IF SOMEONE SEES US?
YOUR MOTHER'LL STEP UP THE...
GRIP
JUST SHUT UP!
...IS IT TRUE YOU WERE MAKING OUT WITH AZUSA?

...HUH...? I DON'T... UNDER-STAND...
vsh
SOMEONE SAW YOU ALL OVER HIM! TOLD EVERYONE YOU'RE A TRAMP...
AND THAT'S WHY THEY'RE BLACKBALLING YOU!
WHAAT ...? NO... WAY...
BUT... I THOUGHT IT WAS YOU.
HUH
ME?!
CUZ I...SAID NO...ABOUT BEING YOUR GIRLFRIEND... SO YOU TOLD YOUR MOM TO...
GIMME A BREAK! YOU THINK I'D GO RUNNING TO MY MOM ?!
BUT! BUT YOU'RE ALWAYS ...
... THREAT-ENING TO TELL YOUR MOM IF I DON'T DO WHAT YOU SAY...
SO...
SO I JUST... ASSUMED ...
This guy...
...really scares me.
Help!
Help ...

HMMMPH

Huh ...?
...COME WITH ME.

WHERE'RE WE GOING? HEY, RYOKI?
COME ON, LET GO OF MY HAND!
RYOKI, I MEAN IT!
Tobishi Trading Higashigaoka Company Housing Complex
WAAAH

DAY CARE ROOM
IT'S MAKING LIFE REALLY HARD FOR US, TOO.
WE DON'T HAVE ANYTHING AGAINST THE NARITAS. WE DON'T WANT TO IGNORE THEM, BUT...
MRS. TACHIBANA CONTROLS THE HIRING AND FIRING AROUND HERE, SO...
Hikaru's such a cutie.

DON'T TELL YOUR MOTHER WE TOLD YOU. PLEASE?
GOSH, I HOPE NONE OF THE OTHER MOMS SAW US.
OF COURSE I WON'T TELL. PROMISE!
SMILE
Glasses removed (sure-fire)
...BUT WHAT STARTED IT OFF IN THE FIRST PLACE?
THEY'RE JEALOUS, THAT'S ALL!
• Mrs. T's henchwomen
a.k.a. The Tachibana Three
THAT HATSUMI-CHAN'S SUCH GOOD FRIENDS WITH THAT GOOD-LOOKING AZUSA.
AT THEIR AGE!
SO THEY STARTED THESE NASTY RUMOURS ABOUT HER AND SPREAD THEM AROUND TO GET MRS. TACHIBANA UPSET.
GLOOM
...THAT IS SO UNFAIR...
THEY COULD'VE TOLD ME WHEN I WENT TO PICK UP HIKARU...
THOSE TWO GIVE ME CHOCOLATES ON VALENTINE'S DAY EVERY YEAR.
...I'M SORRY...
...FOR THINKING IT WAS YOU...

PHEW
BUT GOSH, I'M SO GLAD I KNOW THE REAL REASON NOW.
WHAT A RELIEF...
OKAY, I'M GOING OVER TO YOUR MOM'S TO EXPLAIN THAT IT'S ALL A MISUNDER-STANDING.
I WAS ONLY TALKING TO AZUSA, THAT'S ALL.
YAY, AND THEN THINGS'LL BE...
IT DOESN'T MATTER IF IT'S A MISUNDER-STANDING. NOW THEY THINK YOU'RE A SLUT.
NOTHING YOU SAY IS GOING TO CHANGE THEIR MINDS. IT'S TOO LATE.
YOU ARE SO DUMB.

WHA...
BUT--
BUT I... REALLY DIDN'T... DO ANY-THING... REALLY...
I DIDN'T DO ANYTHING WRONG, SO WHY SHOULD ...?
IT'S NOT JUST ME, IT'S MY WHOLE FAMILY THEY'RE IGNORING.
IT'S NOT FAIR...
THAT'S WHAT YOU GET FOR TALKING TO AZUSA.
MUTTER
I TOLD YOU TO STAY AWAY FROM HIM.
MUTTER
...THEN HOW...
MUMBLE
...CAN I PUT THINGS BACK ...?
...I JUST... DON'T... KNOW WHAT TO DO...

PLOP
WHAT AM I SUPPOSED TO DO...?
I CAN'T TAKE THIS...
Darn it.
I hate saying this in front of him.
WE WERE... JUST...
...LIVING OUR LIVES AND MINDING OUR OWN BUSINESS ...
But ...
WE DIDN'T DO ANYTHING TO DESERVE THIS...SO WHY...DOES THIS HAVE TO HAPPEN TO US? WHY...?
I give up.
I... DON'T KNOW WHAT TO DO...
I CAN'T... TAKE THIS ANY-MORE ...
SOME-BODY... HELP ME...

HEH HEH
...THAT'S RIGHT.
ASK FOR MY HELP.
THAT'S WHAT YOU SHOULD'VE DONE IN THE FIRST PLACE.
HEH
Wha?
COME 'ERE.
Huh?!
I HAVE A GOOD IDEA.
Whaaat?!

WELCOME ...
HEY, UM, RYOKI!
I DON'T... WHAT DO YOU WANT WITH MY BROTHER ?!
AND LET GO OF MY HAND, WILL YOU? HEY.
URGH!
PWIK

RYOKI... TACHIBANA ...
UH... HEY.
YOUR HAND ...
HEY, YOU GO TO...
... HITOTSUBASHI UNIVERSITY, RIGHT? WHAT'S YOUR MAJOR?
DO YOU KNOW ENOUGH MATH TO...
...BE MY PRIVATE TUTOR?
What?!
1401
TACHIBANA

OH, THERE YOU ARE! GOOD. I'D LIKE YOU TO MEET...
...FUTOSHI AYANOKOJI. HE'S A FIRST-YEAR PHYSICS MAJOR AT TOKYO UNIVERSITY, AND I THINK HE'D BE THE IDEAL...
...OH!
ISN'T THAT...THE NARITA BOY...?
MOTHER.
I HAVE A FAVOR TO ASK YOU.

IT'S ABOUT MY NEW TUTOR.
I'D LIKE IT TO BE SHINOGU NARITA HERE.
WHA...
EXCUSE ME?!
WHAT ARE YOU SAYING, DEAR? YOU KNOW WE AGREED LONG AGO...
...THAT ONLY TOKYO UNIVERSITY STUDENTS WOULD DO FOR YOUR TUTOR...
...WELL, I DIDN'T WANT TO TELL YOU THIS, BUT...
YUKA MIZUNO, MY LAST TUTOR, TRIED TO... SEDUCE ME. OF COURSE, I REBUFFED HER ADVANCES...
BUT THAT'S WHY SHE WANTED TO QUIT SO SUDDENLY...
Yeah, right!
GOODNESS GRACIOUS! I HAD NO IDEA!
IN THE MEAN-TIME...
SHINOGU-SAN HAS BEEN HELPING ME OUT WITH THE REALLY DIFFICULT STUFF.
RIGHT?
UH... WELL...
AND THAT'S HOW I GOT TO BE FRIENDS WITH HATSUMI-SAN AS WELL.
MY... I SEE...

IF I HAVE SHINOGU-SAN TUTORING ME UNTIL THE ENTRANCE EXAMS NEXT SPRING...
I'M VERY CONFIDENT...
THAT I WILL BE ACCEPTED INTO TOKYO UNIVERSITY.
GOODNESS...
RYOKI, DARLING ... ♡
URGH! NO WAY!
I UNDERSTAND.
LET'S DO AS YOU SAY, THEN.
SO SORRY, AYANOKOJI-SAN!
Omigod.

Who would ever have thought...
YOU WON'T BELIEVE THIS! DID YOU HEAR?
THE NARITA BOY IS GOING TO BE TUTORING RYOKI TACHIBANA!
WHAAAT?! IS THAT TRUE?
BUNNNN
I ADMIT I HAVE SOME RESER-VATIONS ABOUT IT...
BUT MY SON ABSOLUTELY ***INSISTS*** ON HAVING YOUR SHINOGU-SAN AS HIS TUTOR.
MY! WHAT A TREMEN-DOUS HONOR!!
IF YOU THINK HE'LL BE ADEQUATE, WE'D BE DELIGHTED, OF COURSE!!

GOOD MORNING, MRS. NARITA! ♡
SWARM
SWARM
MRS. NARITA! GOOD MORN-ING!
OH, MRS. NARITA! HOW ARE YOU?
UNBELIEV-ABLE! I MEAN, JEEZ! LOOK AT 'EM...
FALLING OVER THEM-SELVES TO SAY HI TO MOM.
WHAT A DIF-FERENCE A DAY MAKES...
NEVER UNDERESTI-MATE THE POWEFUL POSITION OF "TACHIBANA TUTOR."
YEAH, TOTALLY!! NOBODY'S GONNA BE MEAN TO US NOW.
GREAT IDEA, SHINOGU! YOU'RE SUCH A BRAIN! ♡
...IT WASN'T MY IDEA...
WHAT?! NO WAY.
IT WASN'T?! SO WHOSE WAS IT?
PSHWA
Thank him.
Gotta thank him.

HUFF
HUFF
UM!
UMMM!
GOOD...
GOOD... MORNING...
CHUCKLE
YOU'RE SO EASY TO FIGURE OUT.
IT ENDED, RIGHT? YOU'RE OUT OF THE BIG DEEP FREEZE?
WHAT A BUNCH OF PATHETIC MORONS!

I... WANTED TO THANK YOU...
BECAUSE IT MEANS A LOT TO ME...
...THIS WHOLE THING MIGHT SEEM PATHETIC TO YOU...
BUT TO ME...
...IT'S SUCH A RELIEF NOT TO BE OSTRACIZED ANYMORE. TO HAVE EVERY-THING BACK TO NORMAL.
I'M REALLY GRATE-FUL...
YOU UNDER-STAND WHY...
...I WENT TO ALL THAT TROUBLE TO HELP YOU?
...TO... YOU...
YOU KNOW WHY I DID IT?

PUTTING ON A BIG SHOW FOR MY MOM...
JUST FOR YOU?
KISSING YOUR BROTHER'S ASS...
JUST FOR YOU?
DO YOU UNDER-STAND...
...WHY I WENT TO ALL THAT TROUBLE, JUST FOR YOU?
DO YOU, HATSUMI?

NOD
...BUT, UM...
I...
GOOD.
SO YOU AREN'T AS STUPID AS THAT.

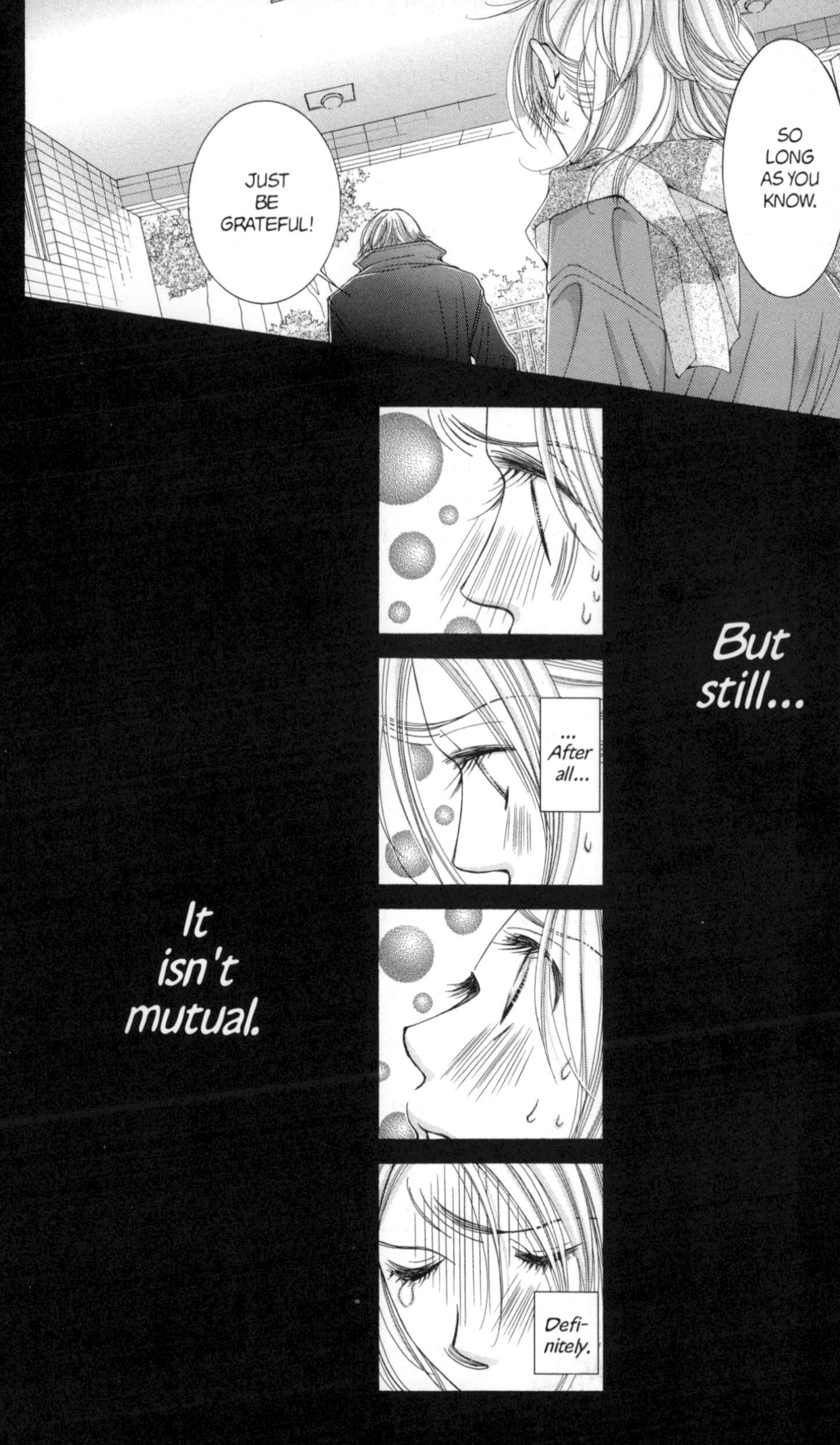
SO LONG AS YOU KNOW.
JUST BE GRATEFUL!
But still...
...After all...
It isn't mutual.
Definitely.

Chapter 17

WHAAAT?! BUT... BUT...

HOW COME?! WHY?! WHY?!

BECAUSE RYOKI WANTS TO COME OVER HERE AND DO IT AT OUR PLACE.

WE CAN'T SAY NO TO THAT.

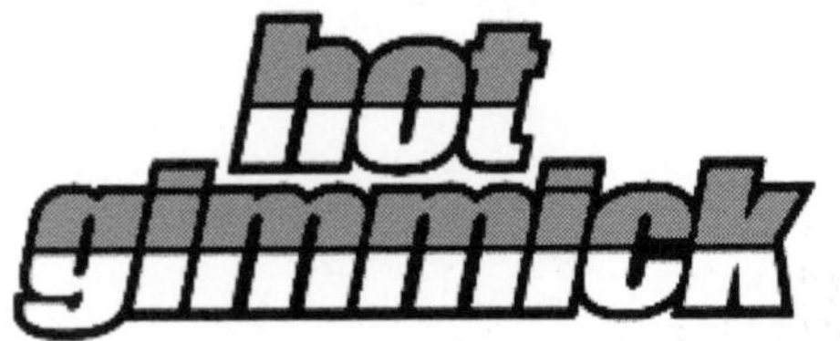

FLUSTER
FLUSTER
FLUSTER
BUT BUT BUT! COME ON!
WHO EVER HEARD OF THE PUPIL GOING TO THE TUTOR'S HOUSE? IT'S SUPPOSED TO BE THE OTHER WAY AROUND!
That's what a tutor does!
SHINOGU HAS TO GO UP TO THE TACHIBANA'S! THAT'S ...
HATSUMI! IT'S NOT SUCH A BIG DEAL. AND IT'S ALREADY DECIDED.
BUT THAT'S JUST NOT...
LOOK, I NEED YOU TO BE HERE. THAT'S WHY I BROUGHT IT UP IN THE FIRST PLACE.
I'M ON THE LATE SHIFT AT WORK ON WEDNESDAYS, SO I WON'T EVEN BE HOME.
WHAAAT?!!
BE NICE AND HOSPITABLE TO HIM, PLEASE?
I'VE HAD MORE THAN ENOUGH OF BEING THE PARIAH AROUND HERE.
WOBBLE
HAVEN'T YOU HAD ENOUGH OF THE SILENT TREAT-MENT?
JUST DON'T GET ON THE WRONG SIDE OF RYOKI TACHIBANA.
PLEASE! HATSUMI ?!

HEY, YA THINK...
...RYOKI WANTS TO COME OVER SO HE CAN BE WITH YOU?
ARE YOU **KIDDING** ?!
I BET HE JUST WANTS TO GO SLUMMING -- TO SEE WHAT LIFE IS LIKE IN THE SHOEBOXES BELOW!
HA HA HA
IT DOESN'T **MEAN** ANY-THING!
...HEY, HATSUMI?
WHAT IS IT ABOUT RYOKI...
...THAT YOU HATE SO MUCH?
WHAT...? WELL... UM...
I MEAN!
HE ACTUALLY LIKES **YOU** BETTER THAN **ME**, OKAY?!
WE'RE TALKING ABOUT RYOKI TACHI-BANA!
HE'S TALL...
HE'S GOOD-LOOKING...
HE'S SMART... HIS LEGS ARE LONG...
ON TOP OF WHICH, HE'S LIKE, THE KING AROUND HERE!!
YOU MAY KISS MY FEET
HAR HAR HAR HAR HAR

PLUS, IF YOU WANNA KNOW WHAT I THINK--
NO WAY. I CAN'T EVEN IMAGINE.
THE BEST WAY TO GET OVER A **LOST LOVE** IS WITH A **NEW** LOVE!
...I CAN'T...
I MEAN...
HE'S TERRIFIED ME SINCE WE WERE LITTLE. AND BEEN MEAN TO ME.
I JUST CAN'T...
NO WAY. THERE'S JUST NO WAY...
I'M GOING AHEAD, OKAY?
HEY, WAIT A--
HA-TSUMI!
...?
SOME-THING'S UP WITH THOSE TWO...
HMPH! I WAS ONLY TRYING TO HELP HER OUT...
DA-DOOM!

Argh, not this one again...
BASH!
HOW OLD ARE YOU, ANY-WAY!?
ARE YOU STUPID ?!
WHY'D MY HEART JUST SKIP A BEAT?!
WORGH
OWWW
I IMAGINED IT! MUST'VE IMAGINED IT!!
BUT THESE ARE GUNDAM ONES.
THEY'RE SUPER-POPULAR RIGHT NOW. I'M COLLEC-TING...
NOT GUNDAM AGAIN?! WHY DON'T YOU JUST GROW UP?!
HE'S A TOTAL DORK! WHY DO I...?!
RYO WOULD NEVER DO SOME-THING LIKE THAT.
I'M NOT TREATING YOU LIKE A KID.
I'M TREATING YOU LIKE A GIRL.

Why ...
...do I think he's kinda cute ?!
Darn ...
That Super Gundam's never gonna come out.
THIS IS RIDICU-LOUS!
OH, THAT'S RIGHT... GLAD I RAN INTO YOU!
YOU'RE REALLY GOOD FRIENDS WITH RYOKI, AREN'T YOU?
DON'T YOU THINK... THAT RYOKI'S PRETTY SERIOUS ABOUT HATSUMI?
GEE... AH...
I ... WELL, I CAN'T REALLY UH...
CUZ IF HE **IS**... *I* THINK...
...MAYBE HE'S THE RIGHT TYPE OF GUY FOR HATSUMI, YOU KNOW?
...

ARE YOU... UH, OKAY NOW?
HUH?
WELL, IT'S JUST...
I THOUGHT YOU...HAD A CRUSH... ON RYO, DIDN'T YOU?
OH, THAT! I'M TOTALLY OVER HIM.
I'M NOT INTO OBSESSING OVER PEOPLE WHO'RE LAME ENOUGH TO REJECT ME!
GRIN
...GOOD. THAT'S GREAT.
I'M GLAD YOU'RE FEELING BETTER.
DA-DOOM!
OH... YEAH?
WELL... SO WHAT?!
WHAT'S IT GOT TO DO WITH YOU, ANYWAY?!
ARGH! SOR...
...RY! I'M SORRY!
EEK!
Oh no.
I did it again.

How come?
Quiver
This sucks. There is no way!
Quiver
I mean, Subaru!
He's a shrimp and a total geek...
He's not even in the picture!
...I'VE DECIDED!
I'M GONNA GET THOSE TWO TOGETHER!
YOU GOTTA HELP ME OUT!
...WHAT? ...WHO, ME?
YEAH, YOU! YOU'RE ONLY, LIKE, HIS BEST FRIEND!
PLUS YOU HAVE NOTHING BETTER TO DO! SO MEET ME IN FRONT OF THOSE GUNDAM MACHINES AT SIX O'CLOCK TONIGHT FOR A STRATEGY SESSION!
BUT... ER...
BUT... I...
SHUT UP! YOU'RE COMING!!
GOT IT?!
Not that...

WEAR MY HAIR DOWN?
WHICH WAY IS CUTER?
...I really want to spend time with Subaru particularly.
AKANE!
THERE'S NO PRACTICE TODAY -- WANNA GO HOME TOGETHER?
LET'S STOP AT THE ARCADE, I HEARD THEY GOT SOME NEW ONES.
HEY, YOU! SHIMADA!
WHO SAYS YOU CAN ASK NARITA OUT, DUDE?
WHO SAYS I CAN'T?
I SAY YOU CAN'T, AW-RIGHT?
PASS ON THAT, SORRY!
I ALREADY HAVE PLANS TODAY.
WHAAT? FOR REAL?!
AKANE, ARE YOU CRAZY?
YOU JUST TURNED SHIMADA DOWN? WHAT A WASTE!
YOU'RE GONNA MAKE ENEMIES, GIRL.
A DUDE?
IS IT A DUDE?
I THOUGHT SHE WAS DUDE-LESS RIGHT NOW.
TOO POPULAR FOR YOUR OWN GOOD.

hotgimmick

WHAT COULD I DO?
I REALLY DO HAVE...
...PLANS TODAY.
Not that ...
...plans with Subaru mean anything to me.
I'M HOME.
This is for Hatsumi. For Hatsumi !!

It's just Subaru anyway. So who cares what I wear?
Any-thing'll do.
And my hair...
ZIP
ZIP
What-ever.
ZIP
What's the hurry?
I MIGHT BE KINDA LATE TODAY!
Don't need to be on time.
SLAM
No biggie if I'm late!
12
11
6
5
HUFF HUFF

THUMP
Jeez ...
Now I feel ...
...more nervous than ever.
THUMP
THUMP
WOW! THIS IS FOR ME?
GOSH! THANKS!
KA-CHANK
...THIS CHANGE WAS WEIGHING ME DOWN.
I WANTED TO GET RID OF IT ANYWAY, IT'S HEAVY.

BRRRING
BRRRING
HELLO, YAGI RESI-DENCE.
SUBA!
FOR YOU. IT'S AKA--
SHH!
DON'T TALK TO ME!
DOO-DOOM
KYUP KYUP
GA-BOOM
I'M TAPING THIS RIGHT NOW. WITH-OUT COMMER-CIALS!
THE VCR'S OUT OF WHACK ALL OF A SUDDEN.
THE TIMER DOESN'T SEEM TO WORK.
AND THERE'S A NEW MOBILE SUIT TODAY...
WOOOW!
THAT IS SO COOL! THAT IS, LIKE, SUPER-INCREDIBLY COOL! TOO MUCH, MAN!
...
WHAT?! CAN'T YOU SEE I'M BUSY?!

THE PHONE. FOR YOU. IT'S AKANE!
EH...? ...
OH CRAP!
OH, MAN! THAT'S RIGHT...
BUP
I don't ...
... believe this.

HUFF
HUFF
I TOTALLY FORGOT I WAS SUPPOSED TO MEET HER...
NOT... HERE... OF COURSE...
OH CRAP...
SHE'S GONNA KILL ME!!
WHEEZE
WHEEZE WHEEZE
...
...BRRR...
HOW DARE YOU BLOW ME OFF
YOU OTAKU TWERP!!
...
Pushover
URGH URGH HELP ME
IT'S... SO UNFAIR...
I... NEVER EVEN SAID I WAS COMING...
PROB'LY DOESN'T MAKE ANY DIFFER-ENCE...
WHO, AKANE?
302
NARITA
NO, SHE'S STILL OUT.

SHE JUST CALLED AND SAID SHE WAS AT THE ARCADE BY THE STATION ...
YOU WANT ME TO CALL HER ON HER CELL PHONE?
NO!! THANKS! SHE'LL REFUSE TO TALK TO ME, FOR SURE.
IT REALLY ISN'T VERY IMPOR-TANT!!
SIGH
?
...COULDN'T EXACTLY TELL HATSUMI THAT IT WAS ABOUT...
...GETTING HER AND RYO TOGETHER...
KA-CHAK
ALL RIGHT! GO, GO!
OH... COME ON!...
AAAAAARGH!

Damn, she's hot. ♡
COME ON, LET ME TRY. I'LL GET YOU THE TEDDY BEAR, PROMISE.
NO! I'M TRYING ONE MORE TIME!
YOU SERIOUS?! I'M OUT OF MONEY, GIRL.
HA HA HA
POOR SHIMADA.
DOES AKANE LIKE TEDDY BEARS SO MUCH, ANYWAY?
YEAH, SHE ONLY CALLED HIM FOR HIS CASH.
wheeeeen
I can't believe it! I can't believe it!!
I can't believe he blew me off. Me!
I even told him ...
...it's for Hatsumi.
BUT... ER...
BUT... I...
For... Hatsumi...

tap
tap
tap
Hatsumi ...
ARGH... I JUST CAN'T... GET IT...
WHAT?! JUST ONE MORE TIME, OKAY?!
HOLD ON A SEC...
OH...
...I'M... SORRY. I, UM...
...MADE YOU WAIT... OUT IN THE COLD... DIDN'T I? I...UH...
I'M REALLY SORRY.
YOU KNOW HIM, AKANE?
HATSUMI SAID YOU WERE HERE, SO...
NO. I DON'T HANG OUT WITH DORKS!

ALL THE BIG GEEK FAVORITES ARE OVER ON THAT SIDE, OKAY?
WHY DON'T YOU HURRY OVER THERE?
I'm so pissed off.
I don't really under-stand why I'm so pissed off...
IF YOU'RE TRYING TO CRUISE HER, SHE'S WITH US, ALL RIGHT?
14-year-old
UH-UH!
16-year-old
YOU GOT THE WRONG IDEA!
SHIMADA! OVER HERE! LET'S PLAY DDR.
OKAY.
But I'm so pissed off.
AKANE, I'LL BE OVER THERE.
OKAY, NO PROB.

...I KNOW WHY YOU DIDN'T COME.
YOU'RE NOT INTO GETTING HATSUMI AND RYOKI TOGETHER, ARE YOU?
CUZ YOU HAVE A CRUSH ON HATSUMI.
WELL... JUST GIVE IT UP!
YOU DON'T EVEN STAND A CHANCE!
AS IF SHE'D PICK YOU OVER RYOKI!
YOU CAN JUST FORGET ABOUT IT!
LOOK AT YOU. YOU'RE BARELY TALLER THAN ME! AND YOU'RE TOTALLY DORKY...

OH...
...I...
...KNOW ALL THAT... ALREADY.

SO... WELL, THAT'S NOT WHY I...
UH... THAT ISN'T... WHAT THIS...
I'M SORRY ...
WHY...
...ARE YOU APOLOGIZING? AFTER WHAT I JUST...
WELL, YOU KNOW.
BECAUSE I STOOD YOU UP TODAY...
BUT LISTEN.
I SWEAR IT WASN'T ON PURPOSE. REALLY.
WHO ...
WHO CARES ?!
I'M GOING !
HUH? AKANE?!

I don't believe him.
APOLOGIZING to me.
When I...
When I...
...made him look like that.

WARGH!
AKANE ?!
WHAT'RE YOU DOING OUT HERE? WHY DON'T YOU GO INSIDE?
HI...
...WHAT'S THE MATTER?
SOME-THING BOTH-ERING YOU?
...WOW. OMIGOD... YOU'RE BEING NICE TO ME...
AS NICE AS YOU ARE TO HATSUMI.
WHA-- C'MON, WHAT'RE YOU TALKING ABOUT?
I'M EQUALLY NICE TO EVERY-BODY!
JUST COME ON INSIDE, AKANE. YOU'LL CATCH A COLD.
GO ON AHEAD. I WANNA SIT HERE A LITTLE LONGER...
If I see Hatsumi now...
...I'll probably lash out at her again.
...OH, THAT'S RIGHT.
JUST NOW, WHEN I WAS GETTING ON THE ELEVATOR...
RUSTLE

HERE.
The one...
YOU GUYS HAVE A FIGHT OR SOME-THING?
...I was trying to...
SUBARU SAID IT'S FOR YOU.
HE SAID TO TELL YOU AGAIN HE WAS SORRY.

...WHEN WAS THAT ...?
HM? OH, LIKE I SAID. JUST NOW.
HEY, AKANE!
DASH
BE BACK IN A SEC! GO ON INSIDE.
SEE YOU LATER!
Jeez ...
5
I'm the one ...
...who should be apolo-gizing.
What is wrong with him ?!
DING DONG
03
YAC

I don't be- lieve him.
OH...
MIN H♥AN LOOK AND LISTEN
SHWA
AGH!
EEK!
SORRY! I'M SORR--
...UH... OH!
THAT'S... UM...
YOU DON'T LIKE IT? IT WASN'T THE ONE YOU WANTED?
...EH?

...IS THIS FOR ME?
I DON'T WANT IT. WHAT WOULD I DO WITH IT?!
I JUST HAD A LOT OF TIME TO KILL TO-NIGHT!
THIS MAKES US EVEN, ALL RIGHT?
YOU DON'T HAVE TO...
I'M GIVING YOU THAT, SO I GET TO KEEP THIS.
OKAY?! IT'S A TRADE...
NO WAY...
AWESOME!
THIS ONE'S ULTRA-RARE!
I DON'T BELIEVE IT! I'VE NEVER SEEN THIS ONE BEFORE!
FLINCH!
WOOOOW!!
THIS IS AMAZING!
CAN I REALLY KEEP IT?! I'M SO STOKED!
THANKS!
...UH... OH.
YOU... WANT IT BACK...?
GUESS SO, HUH? YOU COULD SELL IT FOR A LOT OF MON--
um um...

HUH
...?!

...I LOVE YOU.
KA-PLONK
...EH?
SXWEEEZ
Panic
HUH...?

I WANT YOU TO LOVE ME TOO.
MORE THAN HATSUMI.
...AND MORE THAN GUNDAM!

I'M HOME.
OH HI, SHINOGU.
DID YOU SEE AKANE AROUND?
YEAH, SHE WENT UP TO SUBA-RU'S.
SAID SHE'D BE RIGHT BACK.
OH, OKAY ...
...HEY... SHINOGU ...
YOU KNOW THE TUTORING THING STARTING TOMOR-ROW...
WELL ...
OH YEAH, I HEARD. RYOKI'S COMING OVER HERE FOR THAT, RIGHT?
FINE WITH ME. MAKES LIFE EASIER.
YOU DON'T MIND ?!
...
...HEY, HATSUMI ?
I KNOW YOU SAID YOU TURNED HIM DOWN.
...BUT TELL ME THE TRUTH.
HOW DO YOU HONESTLY FEEL ABOUT RYOKI?

WHAD-DAYA MEAN?
THAT'S EASY.
HE SCARES ME, WHAT ELSE?
...SO YOU DON'T HATE HIM.
YOU'RE **AFRAID** OF HIM?
DON'T HATE HIM...?
I...
OF COURSE I HATE HIM! THAT'S WHY HE SCARES ME!
I MEAN, HE SCARES ME, SO I HATE HIM!
WHY'D YOU ASK ME THAT, ANYWAY?!

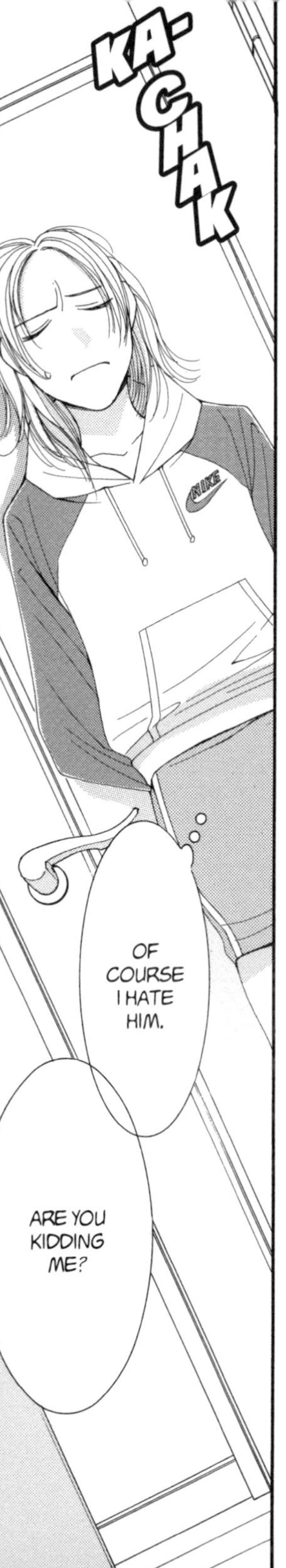

KA-CHAK
OF COURSE I HATE HIM.
ARE YOU KIDDING ME?

...WHY?

THAT'S...

MUMBLE

...BECAUSE I'M JEALOUS...

GODDAMMIT!
RYOKI,
HUH?
HMPH!
RYOKI, JEEZ.
...SHE'S
GOT ME,
DOESN'T
SHE?

Chapter 18

The source of all my woes...

...is the fact that I live in an absolute monarchy*.

*metaphorically speaking

Woe #1
The royal family in our company housing complex...
...is the House of Tachibana.
A slip of the tongue put me in the clutches of the evil Crown Prince...
Scary
Mean
Arrogant
Disagreeable
BE MY SLAVE AND I'LL KEEP QUIET ABOUT IT!
Ryoki Tachibana
Who wanted to do it with me "for practice"...
Made me kiss him (my very first kiss!)...
Groped my breasts...
And was generally making my life miserable, when...
The boy who'd been my first crush moved back to our complex after nine years...
fashion model
Super nice
And came to my rescue, and was really nice to me...
Azusa Odagiri
And we started going out, and were totally in love...
...was what I thought, but...
Woe #2

NOISE ?!
Actually he was only using me...
...as a tool for taking revenge on my dad.
MY MOM WAS BETRAYED BY THE MAN SHE LOVED.
YOUR FATHER. IT KILLED HER.
IT LITERALLY KILLED HER.

WOE #3

While the truth about my dad is still a big mystery...

Just when I was really depressed about being duped by Azusa...

Ryoki Tachibana suddenly tells me...

INSTEAD OF MY SLAVE...
...to be his girlfriend, not his slave.
Which is even worse.
I'LL LET YOU BE MY GIRLFRIEND.

On top of that, when my family was unfairly ostracized by the entire complex...
SO INCONSIDERATE!
I HAVE A FAVOR TO ASK YOU.
He was the one who saved us.

SIGH
DO YOU UNDER-STAND...
WHY I WENT TO ALL THAT TROUBLE, JUST FOR YOU?
DO YOU, HA-TSUMI?
Yeah, but still... the guy scares me.
I don't want to be his girl-friend.
No way. Absolutely not!

I DO APPRECIATE HAVING YOUR SON TUTOR MY RYOKI, MRS. NARITA.

HE'LL BE COMING TO YOUR HOME AT FIVE O'CLOCK TODAY FOR HIS FIRST LESSON.

OH, YES! SHINOGU IS THOROUGHLY COMMITTED TO BEING OF ASSISTANCE!! AREN'T YOU?!

UH...

SOB SOB

Look at them.

Who's tutoring who? You'd think it was the other way around.

POOR SHINOGU ...

*Go out with **that woman's** son? Are you kidding me?*

The fact is, no matter...

rustle rustle

Uh-oh... where are my keys?

...what he does for me, or says to me, I'm never going to feel anything for him except fear. Period.

THUNK

HERE, IT'S A PRESENT.
THIS ISN'T JUST ANY CELL PHONE.
INSTEAD OF JUMPING TO ALL KINDS OF CONCLU-SIONS.
IT'S "FOR MY EARS ONLY."
...I have to give this back to Azusa.
He always used this to call me out...
...for "dates."
ka-chak
But he was just setting me up.
I'm such a fool ...
YOU'RE LATE !!
AS ALWAYS !

WHAT THE HELL TAKES YOU SO LONG, ANYWAY?!
SUBARU TOOK OFF HOURS AGO, JEEZ!
YIPES!
OH...!
IT'S ALL YOUR GODDAMN FAULT IF I'M LATE FOR SCHOOL.
RYOKI... HI...
SO... JUST DON'T WAIT FOR ME, THEN...
MUMBLE
WHAT?!
UH... NOTHING.
GOOD MORNING, I GUESS...
LOOK, YOU GOT SOMETHING TO SAY, JUST COME OUT AND SAY IT! I DON'T HAVE ALL DAY, OKAY?
HUH?
Say WHAT?

What's he talking about?
ER...
UMM... HM?
...STARTING TODAY, I GO OVER TO YOUR PLACE EVERY WEEK, RIGHT?
UH, YEAH...?
BECAUSE I...
...TOLD MY MOM I WANTED YOUR BROTHER TO BE MY TUTOR, RIGHT?
UH, YEAH...?
THANKS TO WHICH, YOU'RE NO LONGER BEING IGNORED BY EVERYONE IN THE COMPLEX.
YOU'RE VERY HAPPY ABOUT THAT. YOU THANKED ME... PROFUSELY.
UH...
YEAH ...?
YOU WERE BESIDE YOURSELF WITH GRATITUDE!
AND NOW YOU'RE DYING TO SAY...
"PLEASE, RYOKI, ALLOW ME TO BE YOUR GIRLFRIEND AFTER ALL."

HAHAHAHAHAHAHA
WELL, IF YOU INSIST... I MEAN, IF YOU'RE BEGGING ME, WELL...
OKAY. SPECIAL OFFER.
AVAILABLE NOW ONLY. YES, I'LL LET YOU BE MY GIRLFRIEND.
...UH... I'M...
... TAKING THE STAIRS ...
HEY!
UM... RYOKI?
IF... I BECAME YOUR GIRLFRIEND, THEN WHAT?
WHADDAYA MEAN, THEN WHAT? WHAT ELSE?
WE DO IT ON A CONSENTING BASIS.
WE KISS AND WE HUG AND WE HAVE SEX SEX SEX SEX!
I KNEW THAT WAS IT!

...BUT... THAT'S NO DIF- FERENT ...
...FROM BEFORE...
HUH ?!
WHAT'RE YOU TALKING ABOUT? THERE'S A HUGE DIF- FERENCE BETWEEN CONSENSUAL AND NON- CONSENSUAL ...
BUT IF THERE ARE NO FEELINGS THERE...
THEN IT'S JUST THE SAME AS BEFORE...
Huh?
...FEELINGS ?
WHADDAYA MEAN ?
YIKES
Uh... oh...

What?!
What did I say?!
Did I say something wrong?!
WELL, UH...I MEAN...
YOU JUST WANT ME TO SHUT UP AND DO WHATEVER YOU SAY, RIGHT?
fluster
fluster
SO...UM, THERE ARE ORDERS I CAN OBEY AND ORDERS I CAN'T OBEY, BUT...
I'LL DO MY BEST TO, WELL, COMPLY WITH YOUR WISHES...
GLANCE
YOU ...
...ARE SO GODDAMN STUPID.
HUH ?!
...FINE. HERE'S AN ORDER FOR YOU.
COME GET ME AT MY PLACE BEFORE FIVE.
WHAT ?!
GO GET YOU? WE LIVE IN THE SAME BUILDING ...
PSHOO
YOU WANNA COMPLY, RIGHT ?!
COFFEE'S GOTTA BE FROM STAR-BUCKS OR I WON'T DRINK IT!

I knew it.
Girlfriend, slave... Same difference.
OKAY, LET'S TAKE ATTENDANCE.
AKITA...
OYAMA...
Only now there's just one **more** reason...
...I have to do what he says.
ODAGIRI... OH RIGHT, HE'S OUT SICK TODAY.
hotgimmick

WHAT? DID YOU SAY AZUSA'S SICK?
YES. THE FLU, APPARENTLY.
KATO...
YEAH, SURE. I BET HE HAD TO GO SOMEWHERE FOR WORK AGAIN.
GUESS WHAT I READ? HE'S GONNA BE IN A TV COMMERCIAL...
UH... HEY, HATSUMI.
DID YOU SEE AZUSA TODAY? IS HE REALLY SICK?
I HAD TO LEAVE THE HOUSE EARLY, SO...
...I DON'T KNOW.
THE TWO OF US AREN'T...
...GOING OUT OR ANYTHING NOW, SO...
How would I know?

I'm the daughter of "the man who killed his mother."
He hates me.
I DON'T SEE AZUSA ANYMORE, SO...

...OH... OOPS... SORRY. I JUST...

WELL, IT'S JUST THAT...

YESTERDAY AT DINNER, MY FOLKS MENTIONED THAT AZUSA'S DAD WAS OUT OF TOWN RIGHT NOW.

AND I WAS THINKING HOW IT'S JUST THE TWO OF THEM, RIGHT?

SO...I WAS WONDERING IF HE'S OKAY, BEING ALONE IN THE HOUSE WHEN HE'S SICK.

WELL... I GUESS AZUSA KNOWS HOW TO TAKE CARE OF HIMSELF, HUH...?

It's got nothing to do with me.

I'M HOME ...
OH...
Guess Shinogu isn't here yet...
Hatsumi - I don't get off work till 7:00 today, so please take good care of Ryoki until I get home. I bought the coffee beans he likes, and some cake to go with. ← These Mom
PATISSIER TAKAGI
ROAST
STARBUCKS COFFEE
COME GET ME AT FIVE!
UGH!
I guess ...
... there's still some time...

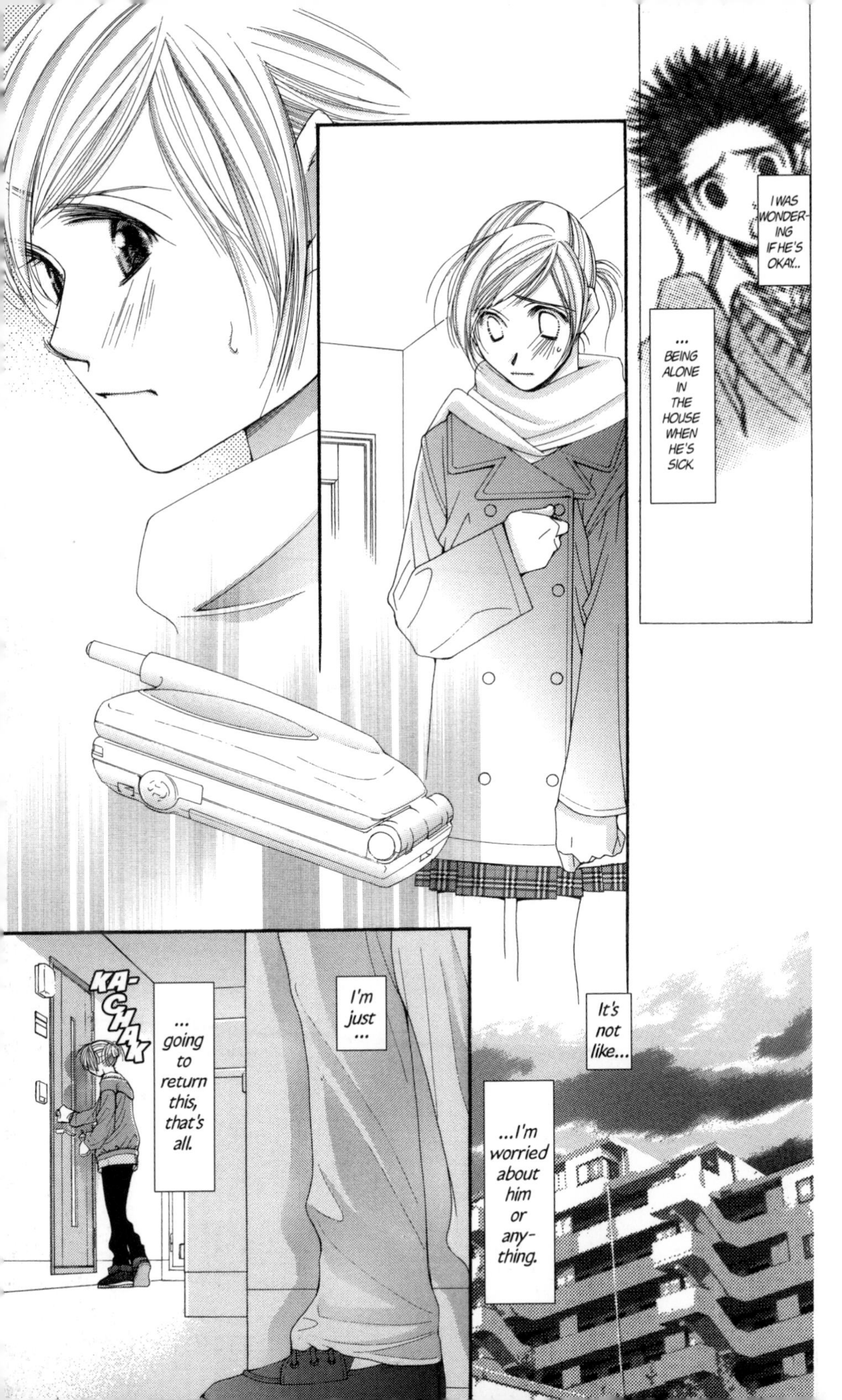
I WAS WONDER-ING IF HE'S OKAY...
... BEING ALONE IN THE HOUSE WHEN HE'S SICK.
It's not like...
...I'm worried about him or any-thing.
I'm just ...
... going to return this, that's all.
KA-CHAK

I'm not worried.
So, okay!!
I just ring the bell ...
...and hand back the cell phone, real quick. And that's it.
I'm not worried.
I'm not worried!!
DINGDONG
Go on, ring it!
...
...YES?

Uh-oh...
...HATSUMI?
...WHAT IS IT...?
His voice is all raspy.
UH... UMM...
705
YOU WERE...OUT SICK TODAY... THE FLU?
NOT THAT I'M WORRIED ABOUT YOU OR ANYTHING! JUST ASKING!
Hey. Calm down, Hatsumi.
I'M HERE ABOUT SOMETHING ELSE.
KLIK
705
ODAGIRI
OH...

I'M TOTALLY FINE, IF YOU WANT THE TRUTH.
JUST FELT LIKE PLAYING HOOKY, THAT'S ALL.
He's lying.
He looks pretty awful.
...
THOUGHT YOU'D FIND ME LYING ON THE FLOOR, MOANING?
SORRY TO DIS-APPOINT YOU.
STOP... BEING SO... STUPID...
IF THAT'S ALL YOU CAME TO SAY...
I'M CLOSING THE DOOR NOW.
WAIT ...!
BAM!
HEY...
He was leaning against the wall the whole time.
He must be really weak.
NO, THAT'S NOT...
IT'S...

THE CELL PHONE! THE ONE YOU GAVE ME.
I BROUGHT IT BACK.
I'M NOT YOUR GIRLFRIEND ANYMORE... OR ANY-THING.
SO... WELL, I DON'T WANT TO KEEP IT.
I'M GIVING IT BACK, SO OPEN THE DOOR. COME ON.
...
...DID YOU...
...GO SEE A DOCTOR ...?

I HEARD YOUR DAD'S OUT OF TOWN.
HAVE YOU BEEN EATING AT ALL?
SLIDE
YOU WON'T GET BETTER IF YOU DON'T EAT.
YOU'RE SUCH A SAP, HATSUMI.
IF YOU COME NEAR ME, YOU'RE JUST GONNA GET DUPED AGAIN.
SO JUST GO AWAY, WILL YOU?
...I CAN'T JUST GO AWAY. YOU'RE SICK.
COME ON, OPEN UP.
I WISH I COULD... BUT I CAN'T. YOU'RE AN OLD FRIEND. I CAN'T JUST WALK AWAY.
TOO BAD. I'M NOT LETTING YOU IN.

I DON'T WANT THE DAUGHTER OF THAT SCUMBAG TAKING CARE OF ME.
...JUST THROW IT OUT. THE CELL PHONE.
I DON'T CARE...

YOU WANNA HELP ME OUT, TELL ME WHEN YOUR DAD'S COMING BACK NEXT.
I THINK THIS TIME I'LL GO OVER TO YOUR PLACE FOR A BIG SHOWDOWN ...
SCREW YOU, AZUSA !!
TA TA TA TA
SLUMP SLUMP
SIGH

...REVENGE. YEAH, RIGHT.
ALL I'M DOING IS HURTING HATSUMI, THAT'S ALL...
WHAT AN ***ASS-HOLE***...

KA-PLONK
WHOOPS ...
THWOK
HEY...!

LIKE HE SAID, THROW IT OUT!
I TOLD YOU TO STAY AWAY FROM THAT BASTARD!
WHEN THE HELL ARE YOU GOING TO LEARN?!
YOU... YOU WERE WATCHING ...?
I TOLD YOU TO COME GET ME!

SHWA
BUT... BUT IT WASN'T TIME YET...
SHUT UP.
COME 'ERE!
KLAK
KA-CHAK!
...YOU SAID THE WAY IT WAS BEFORE ...
...WAS FINE WITH YOU.

YOU DIDN'T WANT TO BE MY GIRLFRIEND...
BUT YOU'D BE MY SLAVE...
...AND DO WHATEVER I WANTED. RIGHT?
UH...
GRRIP
OW...
OUCH...!
THAT HURTS, RYOKI!
SHUT UP!
YOU SAID YOU'D OBEY ME, REMEMBER?

STOP WORRYING ABOUT THAT GODDAMN AZUSA.

DON'T EVER GO OVER TO HIS HOUSE AGAIN.
DON'T EVEN THINK ABOUT HIM, EVER.
...AND NOT JUST AZUSA--
THAT GOES FOR ANY GUY OTHER THAN ME.
THAT'S AN ORDER.

...IF YOU CAN OBEY THAT...
...I'LL LET YOU BE MY SLAVE, INSTEAD OF MY GIRLFRIEND.
YOU...
RYOKI...?
YOU KNOW WHAT YOU SAID THIS MORNING?
THAT THERE ARE FEELINGS THERE.

WELL, I...
I'M SAYING YOU'RE THE ONE I WANT.
I HATE IT WHEN YOU WORRY ABOUT SOMEONE ELSE.
IT DRIVES ME CRAZY TO SEE YOU TOUCH OR TO BE TOUCHED MY SOMEONE ELSE.
I CAN'T EVEN STAND SEEING YOU SMILE AT SOMEONE ELSE.
I JUST CAN'T STAND IT!

THE FEELINGS ARE THERE. YOU'RE JUST IGNORING THEM.
DA-DOOM

DA-
DOOM!
DA-
DADOOM!

DA-DOOM

DA-DOOM
tok tok tok tok
KA-CHAK
WOPE!
YOU SCARED ME.
HI...
DA-DOOM
DA-DOOM
DA-DOOM
HI. SORRY I'M A BIT LATE.
DA-DOOM

UH... MY ROOM'S OVER HERE, SO...
CAN YOU WAIT IN HERE?
HA-TSUMI? WOULD YOU MIND GETTING US SOME COFFEE ?
HATSUMI ?
FWA
WHY'RE YOU JUST STANDING THERE? YOU OKAY?
OH. YEAH. I'M FINE.
SORRY.
KLAK

DOOM
COFFEE. COFFEE. RIGHT. OKAY.
DA-DOOM
UH...
GOOD LUCK, SHINOGU.
HATSUMI?
DA-DOOM
...WHAT'S UP? YOU'RE ACTING FUNNY.
DON'T TELL ME HE SCARED YOU AGAIN. WHAT DID HE DO?
NO...!
NO, HE DIDN'T SCARE ME, HE...
HM...?
UH, NO-THING!
IT'S NOTHING, REALLY,
I'LL BRING THE COFFEE IN A SEC!
KLAK
He didn't scare me...

He made my heart throb.

Chapter 19

"THAT GOES FOR ANY GUY OTHER THAN ME."

DA-DOOM

"YOU'RE THE ONE I WANT."

DA-DOOM

DA-DOOM

DA-DOOM

DA-DOOM!

Oh my god. This is crazy.

I just can't ...
...get that out of my head.
YOU MORON!
I mean, come on, Hatsumi.
It's Ryoki Tachibana!
You've always been terrified of him.
standing
sitting
lying down
Though today he was different from usual.
Omigod! What is going on? This is nuts!!
DA-DOOM
I've never felt like this.
KLIK
Ryoki? Making my heart throb? It just isn't possible.
This is too weird ...

SILENCE
Tutor
Pupil
"No. He didn't scare me, he ..."
...I GUESS... SOMETHING HAPPENED BETWEEN THEM...
FROM THE WAY HATSUMI WAS BLUSHING ...
GLANCE
OOPS
UH... HA HA! UMM!
WHERE DO YOU WANT TO START? THE UH, LESSON...
YOUR MOTHER SAID TO CONCENTRATE ON MATH AND SCIENCE, SO...
HAVE YOU TAKEN ANY CALCULUS YET?
YOU DON'T HAVE TO TEACH ME ANY-THING.

University Testing Center Preliminary Examination Student Report
Practice University Entrance Examination Student Report
Math 1/2 (200 pts)
Japanese(200pts) Japanese I II
English - Math - Japanese Total
Science (100 pts each)
Physics 1B
Chemistry 1B
School of Preference
1 Tokyo University
2 Tokyo University
3 Tokyo University
HUH ...?
FLIK
NONE OF MY OTHER TUTORS EVER DID EITHER. SO JUST RELAX.
...WELL, YOU GET THE GENERAL IDEA.
I DON'T PARTICULARLY NEED ANY HELP IN MATH OR SCIENCE.
...
...SO WHY'D YOU WANT ME TO BE YOUR TUTOR, THEN...?
First time he's seen better scores than his own.

SO I CAN BE WITH YOUR SISTER.
THIS WAY, IT WON'T BE SO STRANGE IF I SPEND TIME WITH HER.
SO ANYWAY.
HOW YOU USE THESE TWO HOURS EVERY WEDNESDAY IS UP TO YOU.
...ARE YOU...
... SERIOUS ABOUT HATSUMI?

SHOULD THAT BE...
...ANY CONCERN OF YOURS?
I'M HOOOME!
SO? EVERYTHING OKAY? HE'S HERE, RIGHT?! I SAW EXPENSIVE SHOES IN THE ENTRANCE!!
DID YOU MAKE THE COFFEE?! DID YOU SERVE THE CAKE?! IS EVERYTHING OKAY?!
UH, YEAH. I DID EVERYTHING YOU SAID...
Actually...
Everything's not okay, but that's...
OH GOOD!! I WAS WORRIED SICK...
OH! WHICH REMINDS ME! I WAS ALSO WORRIED ABOUT...

...AZUSA! HE MISSED SCHOOL TODAY?
I HEARD HE'S RUNNING A FEVER.
UM... YEAH...
HIS FATHER'S AWAY ON A BUSINESS TRIP, APPARENTLY. HE MUST BE ALL ALONE IN THAT APARTMENT!
WE CAN'T JUST LEAVE HIM TO HIS OWN DEVICES. OUR NEIGHBORS ALL AGREE ABOUT THAT.
Mom ...
...doesn't seem to know anything about... Dad and Azusa.
SO HATSUMI ...
I'M GOING TO MAKE HIM SOME PORRIDGE.
AND I WANT YOU TO TAKE IT OVER THERE WHEN IT'S READY, OKAY?
NO! NO NO NO! NOT ME! NO CAN DO!
HATSUMI! WE ALL HELP EACH OTHER HERE.
I KNOW, BUT I'M THE WRONG PERSON!
DON'T TELL ME. YOU'RE EMBARRASSED BECAUSE YOU'LL SEE HIM IN HIS PAJAMAS?! (tee hee)
I already went over there. And he wouldn't let me in!
KLAK
I'D LIKE TO GO WITH YOU.

I'M REALLY WORRIED ABOUT AZUSA, TOO... (big lie)
THAT'S AN ORDER!
SHALL WE GO THERE TOGETHER, HATSUMI?
BWOFF
OH, RYOKI-KUN! HOW SWEET OF YOU!
UH...
YESSIR!
SURE, OKAY...
HOW WAS THE LESSON?
I HOPE SHINOGU WAS ALL RIGHT. WAS HE ABLE TO EXPLAIN THINGS CLEARLY?
OH YES! VERY CLEARLY.
HE HELPED ME A GREAT DEAL.
RIGHT, SHINOGU-SAN?

...WELL.
I... REALLY DIDN'T DO MUCH AT ALL ...
I'M SO GLAD THIS IS WORKING OUT!
HOO HOO HOO
Urgh... He does scare me... The guy totally scares me.
I must've just imagined my heart throbbing.
Yeah. That's what it was. I imagined it!!
AND PLEASE BE SURE TO GIVE YOUR MOTHER MY BEST REGARDS, RYOKI-KUN!
OH YES, OF COURSE.
TUMP!
OH, SOR... SHINOGU ...? WHATSA MATTER?
YOU SEEM KINDA OUT OF IT. YOU OKAY?
DID THAT TUTORING SESSION TIRE YOU OUT?
SHINOGU ...?

YEAH, I'M FINE.
WHAT ABOUT YOU? YOU DON'T HAVE TO GO OVER TO AZUSA'S, YOU KNOW...
...WELL... I GUESS IF RYOKI'S WITH YOU... YOU'LL BE ALL RIGHT...

SLAM
Shinogu ...?

Some-thing ***IS*** *bother-ing him, isn't it...?*

...NO.
NO.
HOLD IT IN.
...YOU GOTTA HOLD IT IN, COME ON.
YOU CAN'T ...
SO...

HOW COME SO MANY PEOPLE NEED TO GO? (pissed off)
WHAT IS THIS, THE CANDYSTRIPER BRIGADE?
NO... UH... WELL...
SUBARU WAS REALLY WORRIED ABOUT AZUSA, RIGHT?!
Sorry, Ryo!
AND AKANE...UH, IS HELPING ME CARRY THE FOOD!
...
FINE, WHAT-EVER.
WE'RE JUST TAKING THE STUFF OVER AND COMING RIGHT BACK ANYWAY!
HURRY UP! WE'RE GOING!
HEY, WAIT!
Doesn't offer to carry her stuff
WE CAN'T JUST DUMP IT AND GO. WE HAVE TO SEE HOW HE IS!
HE SEEMED REALLY FEVERISH ...
I TOLD YOU TO STOP WORRYING ABOUT HIM!
YOU DOPE!
BONK!

MUTTER MUTTER

BUT... MY MOM SAID TO...

IF HE HATES AZUSA SO MUCH, WHY'D HE COME?!

...FER CHRISSAKE. I KNOW HOW YOUR MIND WORKS.

YOU'RE AFRAID OF GOING OVER THERE ALONE AND HAVING AZUSA SLAM THE DOOR IN YOUR FACE AGAIN.

PA-THETIC!

WHAT DOES AZUSA HAVE, THE FLU?

DOES HE HAVE A HIGH FEVER OR SOME-THING?

THUMP!

GEE, UH... I DON'T REALLY KNOW.

I S-STOPPED BY THERE AFTER SCHOOL, B-BUT HE SEEMED TO BE ASLEEP.

HOPE HE G-GETS BET-TER SOON!

BUMBLE

BUMBLE

...YOU DON'T HAVE TO FREAK OUT.
I'M NOT GONNA JUMP ON YOU ANYMORE...
YOU'VE BEEN STEERING CLEAR OF ME EVER SINCE, HAVEN'T YOU?
YOU LEAVE EARLY EVERY MORNING SO WE WON'T SEE EACH OTHER.
WHEN YOU TRY SO HARD TO AVOID SOMEBODY...
...IT HURTS THEIR FEELINGS.
AKA...
HEY, HATSUMI, WAIT UP!
...HATSUMI.
YIKES
WHAT...?
LOOK WHO'S HERE.
DING DONG
It's her...

KA-CHAK
MY GOD... LOOK AT YOU. WHAT'S YOUR TEMPERATURE?
RINA... COME ON IN.
YOU NEED TO EAT SOMETHING AZUSA.
"RINA...
"COME ON IN."
...OH.
OH... HATSUMI-SAN.
GOOD EVENING. I JUST CAME TO CHECK ON AZUSA.
I...
...GUESS YOU'RE ALL HERE FOR THE SAME REASON.

NICE TO MEET YOU. I...MY NAME IS RINA KATSURAGI.
I RUN THE MODELING AGENCY THAT REPRESENTS AZUSA.
I GUESS YOU COULD SAY I'M HIS MANAGER...
I'M NOT LETTING YOU IN.
I DON'T WANT...
...THE DAUGHTER OF THAT SCUM-BAG...
...TAKING CARE OF ME.
OMI-GOD
NO WAY! FOR REAL?! YOU RUN THE WHOLE AGENCY?
THAT'S SO COOL!
I MEAN MY GOD, YOU'RE SO YOUNG!
UM, THANKS, I GUESS, BUT I'M REALLY NOT VERY YOUNG...
KOFF KOFF
KOFF
AZUSA! YOU BETTER GO INSIDE AND GET BACK INTO BED.
WELL, IF YOU'LL EXCUSE US...

UH... UM.
GREAT! SO, UM, I'M GLAD AZUSA'S IN SUCH GOOD HANDS!
THIS IS SOME PORRIDGE MY MOM MADE FOR HIM, AND...
THERE'S LOTS OF FOOD HERE FROM SUBARU'S MOM TOO.
WE ONLY CAME BY BECAUSE WE KNEW AZUSA'S DAD WAS AWAY.
BUT NOW THAT ***YOU'RE*** HERE, RINA-SAN, HE ISN'T ALONE ANYMORE, SO...
PHEW! THAT'S A RELIEF!

He doesn't mind having Rina take care of him.

COME ON, RYOKI. LET'S GO HOME!
HUH? UH. YEAH...
LET'S GO, OKAY?!
QUEEZE
BYE, AZUSA! HOPE YOU GET BETTER SOON!
AKANE, WE'RE GOING.
BYE, AZUSA-KUN! AND NICE TO MEET YOU, RINA-SAN!
I'M AKANE NARITA AND I LIVE ON THE THIRD FLOOR OF THIS BUILDING! I'M FOURTEEN! AKANE NARITA!
...

SCREW YOU, AZUSA.
...
...AZUSA, GET INSIDE! IT'S COLD OUT HERE.
...HEY, THAT TALL BOY?
HE ISN'T HATSUMI-SAN'S... BOYFRIEND... IS HE? BECAUSE I THOUGHT...
CAN YOU CLOSE THE DOOR, RINA?
KLAK

HATSUUUMEE! HURRY, HURRY!
WE CAN'T HOLD THE ELEVATOR FOREVER!
COME ON, YOU GUYS!
RYOKI-KUN!
...
...GO AHEAD WITHOUT US, NARITA JUNIOR.
Doesn't remember her name
HATSUMI AND I HAVE TO TALK. WE'LL COME LATER.
JU... JUNIOR ?!!

DING
...PHEW?
WHAT A RELIEF, RINA-SAN? WE'RE SO GLAD YOU'RE HERE?
YEAH, RIGHT.
WHO'D YOU THINK YOU WERE KIDDING? YOU ARE SO STUPID!
...I KNOW, BUT... WHEN HE...
WHEN I SAW AZUSA OPEN THE DOOR TO LET HER IN...
I FELT... SO JEALOUS...
I KNOW I'M STUPID... I KNOW THERE'S NO WAY, BUT I STILL...
WHY DID THAT HURT SO MUCH...?

...YOU ARE STUPID...
BUT YOU DID PUT UP A BRAVE FRONT BACK THERE.
I'LL GIVE YOU THAT.

BUT...
STILL TOO MUCH AZUSA.
BONK!
BYE...
I'M GOING HOME.
WE LIVE IN OPPOSITE DIRECTIONS, SO...BYE.
DA-DOOM
DA-DOOM
Oh no.

DA-DOOM
DA-DOOM
Here it is again.
SEE YA.
Omi-god.
DA-DOOM
My heart's pounding...
Over Ryoki.
DA-DOOM

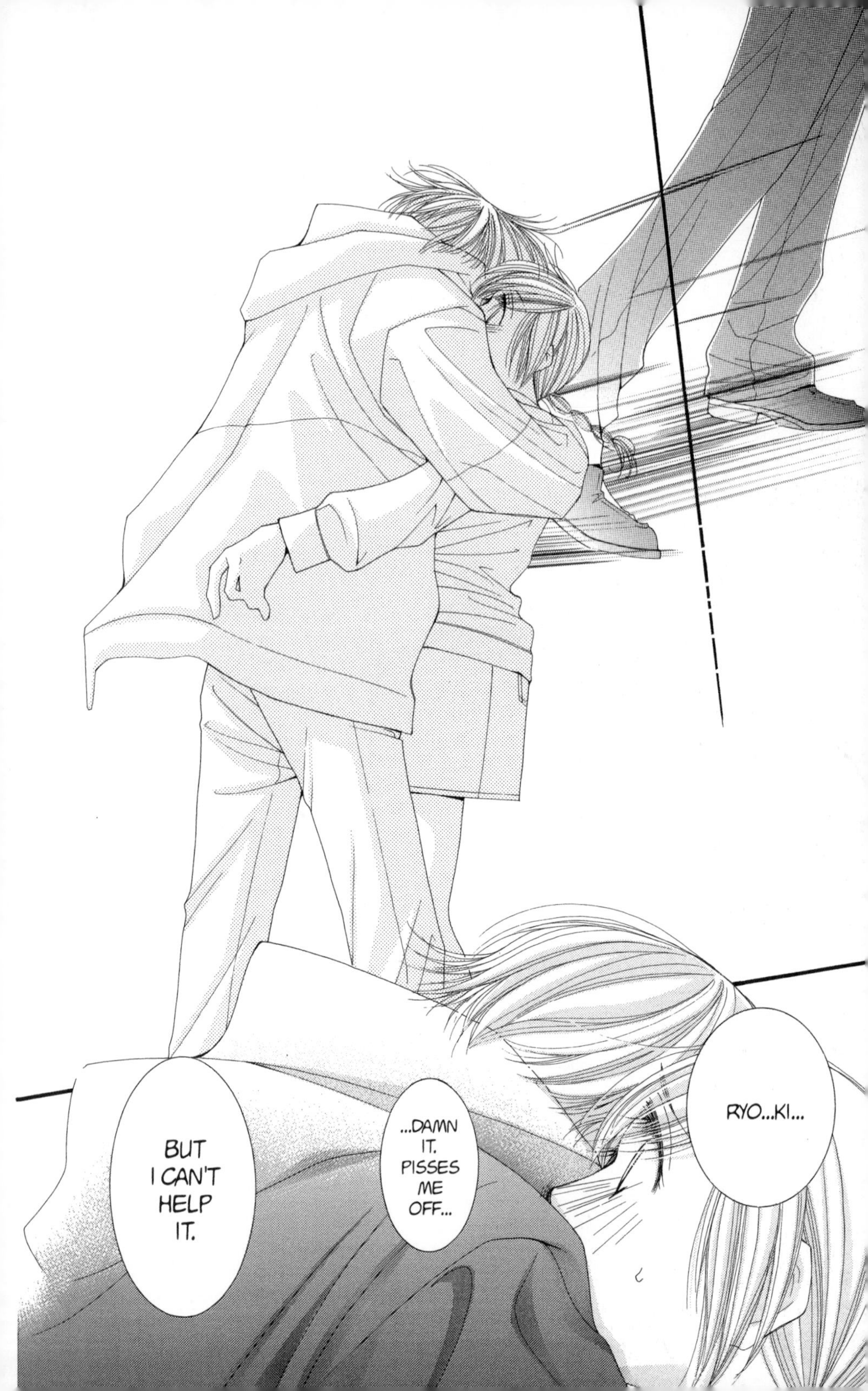
RYO...KI...
...DAMN IT. PISSES ME OFF...
BUT I CAN'T HELP IT.

YOU'RE SO DAMN CUTE!
PHWOOSH

DA-DOOOM!
SHOVE
I-I'M TAKING THE STAIRS.
HEY! HATSU...
GOOD NIGHT! GOOD NIGHT, BYE!
DA-DOOOM
What is this?
My heart's just flipping out.
DA-DOOOM

HATSUMI...
SHINOGU!!
kyuween
WHAT'S UP...?
DID AZUSA SAY SOME-THING MEAN TO YOU?

Oh no.
NO... IT'S NOT THAT.
I DON'T...
Seeing Shinogu's face makes me feel...
...so relieved...
That every-thing I'm feeling...
...is about to come spilling right out.
WHAT ABOUT YOU, SHINOGU? WHAT ARE YOU DOING OUT HERE?
IT'S COLD. YOU'LL GET SICK.
OH...
SHOULD THAT BE...
ANY CON-CERN OF YOURS?
I WAS JUST...
...COOLING MY HEAD OFF...
YOUR HEAD?!

YOU FEEL FEVERISH ?! OMIGOD, MAYBE YOU HAVE THE FLU TOO?
YOU SHOULDN'T BE OUT HERE! C'MON, LET'S GO INSIDE.
NO, NO. I'M NOT SICK.
tump
HEY, I ASKED YOU A QUESTION.
WHAT DID AZUSA SAY TO YOU?
DAMN IT, I'M NOT KEEPING QUIET ANYMORE IF HE...
NO...
THAT'S NOT...
I ... OMIGOD, SHINOGU... I ...

SOME-THING'S THE MATTER WITH ME...
...
...
...FER CHRIS-SAKE!
SHWA
WHAT'M I SUP-POSED TO THINK...
... WHEN SHE RUNS OFF LIKE THAT?!
PISSES ME OFF!
I ... MY HEART STARTS POUNDING... I DON'T KNOW...
I MEAN, RYOKI TACHIBANA... I'VE ALWAYS HATED HIM...
THE GUY TERRIFIES ME...

"ARE YOU SERIOUS ...
"...ABOUT HATSUMI ?"
I DON'T KNOW WHAT'S THE MATTER WITH ME...
Should that be...
...THIS IS... CRAZY... RIGHT? IS SOMETHING WRONG ...
...WITH ME?
THE HIGH AND MIGHTY RYOKI TACHIBANA ...
I MEAN, YOU'VE GOT TO BE KIDDING ME, RIGHT?
SORRY!! I DON'T KNOW WHAT'S WRONG WITH ME.
FORGET WHAT I JUST SAID!
...any concern of yours?

ALL I KNOW IS...
...IT CONCERNS ME.
Goddamn it.

Hot Gimmick

vol.5

MIKI AIHARA

Chapter 20

DEAR GOD, FORGIVE ME.
I ...
I'M IN LOVE WITH MY OWN SISTER.

I SWEAR I'LL NEVER, EVER TELL ANYONE.
I PROMISE TO KEEP IT A SECRET.
SO PLEASE...
PLEASE...
PLEASE, GOD...
SHINOGU...?

PLEASE LET HATSUMI...
...ALWAYS BE WITH ME, FOREVER AND EVER.
PLEASE...
...
LET HATSUMI BE MINE ALONE.

SHINOGU...? WHAT'S UP?
HEY... YOU ARE FEELING SICK, AREN'T YOU?
YOUR HEAD HURTS? MAYBE IT'S THE FLU.
HEY... SHINOGU?
YOU OKAY?
LOUDER, DAMN IT!
I CAN'T HEAR YOU.
...IT'S LOVE.
HUH...?

YOUR HEART POUNDING AND STUFF.
SPEAK UP...
YOU'RE TRYING TO TELL YOURSELF IT ISN'T TRUE, THAT SOME-THING'S WRONG WITH YOU, BUT...
IT SEEMS TO ME...
...THAT YOU'RE FALLING IN LOVE WITH RYOKI, HATSUMI.
I CAN'T HEAR A DAMN THING.
WHA... AS IF!
YOU ARE SO DENSE, HATSUMI.
NO I'M NOT! I MEAN, COME ON! THERE IS NO WAY...
I CAN TELL...

BECAUSE I LOVE YOU.
...HEY...! WHAT...
WHAT'RE YOU TALKING ABOUT? COME ON, SHINOGU. DON'T BE SO... GOSH!
You're embarrassing me...
OF COURSE YOU LOVE ME! CUZ YOU'RE MY BROTHER, RIGHT?

I DON'T KNOW! SOMETHING'S WRONG WITH YOU. I THINK YOU NEED TO GET INSIDE AND GO TO BED!
I BET IT'S BECAUSE YOU'RE FEVERISH THAT YOU'RE SAYING ALL THIS WEIRD STUFF.
SHWA
There is no way I would fall in love with Ryoki.
THERE'S... NO WAY...
...THAT WOULD EVER HAPPEN...
Come on, Hatsumi.
Ryoki Tachibana is a mean, nasty creep who orders you around, remember?

...WHAT THE HELL WAS THAT?
Don't get all nervous and excited around him...
...just because he was kinda nice (?) to you for a change.
Don't. Don't! DON'T!

Look what happened when you fell for Azusa.
I'm not getting carried away like that again. I'm not walking into another trap...
No way.
OKAY.
FUMBLE FUMBLE
I'M GOING...
WAIT, HATSUMI! HATSUMI! HANG ON...
SSSHHH! MOM!
SHINOGU'S SICK. YOU'LL WAKE HIM UP!
HUH?

WHAT'RE YOU TALKING ABOUT? SHINOGU LEFT THE HOUSE AGES AGO.
HE SAID HE HAD AN EARLY-MORNING CLASS TODAY.
HE SEEMED FINE TO ME. WHO SAID HE'S SICK?
Huh...?
So I guess he's okay.
But he was acting really strange yesterday.
ANYWAY, HERE.
I GOT THESE FROM A FRIEND AT WORK.
OH...
THEY'RE FOR YOU. DON'T TELL AKANE -- SHE HAS TO STUDY FOR NEXT WEEK'S MIDTERMS.
THEY'RE TWO TICKETS TO THE MOVIES.
PLUS, YOU WERE SUCH A GREAT HELP TO ME YESTERDAY WHEN RYOKI WAS HERE.

...WHAT'S EATING HIM THIS MORNING ...?
COMES TO PICK ME UP FOR A CHANGE, AND THEN DOESN'T SAY A WORD...
SUBARU.
YARGH!
GYAK!
...I DON'T HAVE ANY SO I WOULDN'T KNOW, BUT...
DO BROTHERS AND SISTERS GO AROUND HUGGING EACH OTHER ALL THE TIME?

OR, TO BE MORE SPECIFIC, DO YOU GO AROUND HUGGING ASAHI? LIKE, REAL TIGHT?
NOT JUST THAT...
BUT SAYING STUFF LIKE "BECAUSE I LOVE YOU" TO HER, LIKE AS IF YOU'RE HER BOYFRIEND OR SOME-THING?
AS IF! OF COURSE NOT!!
I MEAN, SHE PRACTICES WRESTLING HOLDS AND STUFF ON ME ALL THE TIME...
BUT COME ON, NOBODY GOES AROUND SAYING "I LOVE YOU" TO THEIR SISTER...
...THAT'S WHAT I THOUGHT ...
WHAT? WHY'D YOU ASK ME THAT, ANYWAY?
UGH... GROSS!
JUST THINKING ABOUT IT CREEPS ME OUT.
"I love you"
Hug
Shinogu
Discomfort index
ALTHOUGH MY IGNORANCE OF NORMAL SIBLING BEHAVIOR PREVENTED ME FROM DRAWING A DEFINITE CONCLUSION REGARDING THE LEGITIMACY OF WHAT I OBSERVED...
MY FEELINGS OF DISCOMFORT, ON A SCALE OF 1 TO 10, WERE UP THERE AROUND 26 AND RISING...
WHAT THE HELL ARE YOU TALKING ABOUT...?

hotgimmick

OH-- SORRY, HATSUMI!
I ALREADY SAW THAT ONE WITH MY BOY-FRIEND.
IT WAS REALLY GOOD. YOU SHOULD TOTALLY GO.

OH... YOU'VE BOTH SEEN THIS MOVIE?
YEAH, I JUST SAW IT SUNDAY WITH MY MOM. I LIKED IT A LOT.
OH WELL... THAT'S TOO BAD.
GUESS I'LL GET MY BROTHER TO GO WITH ME, AS USUAL...
WHAT'S "TOO BAD" ABOUT THAT?!
YOUR BROTHER'S A TOTAL BABE! I'M SO JEALOUS!
PUNCH
YEAH. LUCKY YOU, HATSUMI.
WHY DON'T YOU GO WITH RYOKI?
AZUSA!
SQUEAL
ARE YOU OKAY NOW?
SQUEAL
YEAH. I'M FINE.
GOSH, WE WERE ALL SO WORRIED ABOUT YOU! ♡
smile
THANKS.

HEY, HEY...WHAT WAS THAT ABOUT JUST NOW?
WHO'S THIS "RYOKI" YOU WERE TALKING ABOUT?
HM? OH, THAT'S HATSUMI'S CURRENT BOYF--
NOOOO! HE IS NOT!
YANK!
YOU'RE STILL FEVERISH! I THINK YOU NEED TO GO SEE THE NURSE, NOW! COME ON!!
...UH... M...
TELL YOUR MOM THANKS FOR MAKING THAT FOOD FOR ME.
THAT'S NOT...LOOK, DON'T SAY STUFF LIKE THAT IN FRONT OF EVERYBODY, OKAY?
BUT ...
WHEN YOU LEFT MY PLACE YESTERDAY, AFTER BRINGING THE FOOD...
YOU WERE HOLDING ON TO RYOKI'S SLEEVE THE WHOLE TIME.
CLUTCHING IT REAL TIGHT, LIKE YOU WERE TOGETHER.

NO I WASN'T! THERE'S NO WAY!
HM...?
YOU SAYING IT WAS UNCON-SCIOUS?
No way.
BLUSH
I couldn't have been.
NO-THING WRONG WITH IT.
I DONT KNOW... RYOKI SEEMS TO HAVE FALLEN PRETTY HARD FOR YOU.
WHA... COME ON, YOU'VE GOTTA BE...
GO AHEAD AND BE HIS GIRL-FRIEND, WHY DONCHA?
YOU'LL NEVER BE BLACKBALLED AT THE COMPLEX AGAIN, THAT'S FOR SURE.
OH... IS THAT IT...

SURE. GO OUT WITH **HIM**, AND THERE'S LOTS OF FRINGE BENEFITS, AREN'T THERE?
I **THOUGHT** IT WAS STRANGE. I MEAN, YOU WERE TOTALLY TERRIFIED OF THE GUY WHEN WE WERE LITTLE.
NOW I GET IT. YOU'RE LOOKING OUT FOR YOURSELF, AREN'T YOU?
...
WHAT ...?
WHY DO YOU HAVE TO BE SO MEAN TO ME?
...I... WOULD NEVER DATE SOMEONE FOR A REASON LIKE THAT.
BUT... EVEN IF I **WERE** GOING OUT WITH RYOKI, FOR ANY REASON, IT'S NONE OF YOUR BUSINESS ANYWAY.

BZZZZZZ
BZZZZZZ
BZZZZZZ
...YOU'RE RIGHT.
I WONDER WHY?
Hello?!
WHAT'S THAT SUPPOSED TO MEAN?!
HEY, YOU TWO OVER THERE!
IT'S TIME FOR CLASS.
GET INSIDE. MOVE IT!
UH, RIGHT! WE'RE COMING.
...MAYBE CUZ... I DON'T LIKE IT.

CUZ IF YOU HAVE RYOKI BEHIND YOU...
IT'LL BE HARDER FOR ME TO GET BACK AT YOUR DAD.
HE ISN'T BEHIND ME, OKAY?!
ROLL...
KLATTER
KLATTER
YOU WERE HOLDING ON TO RYOKI'S SLEEVE.
CLUTCHING IT REAL TIGHT THE WHOLE TIME.
LIKE YOU WERE TOGETHER.
...I'm sorry, but I don't remember doing that!

No way.
I did no such thing.
I couldn't have.
I mean, come on...
If I did...
...that would mean...
TOKIWA DRUGS

I feel...
...protected by him...
YES, MY LOYAL SUBJECT.
MY LORD...
WAAAARGH!
TMP
...WHAT'S YOUR PROBLEM?
IF YOU'RE GONNA MAKE SO MUCH NOISE, DO IT SOMEWHERE ELSE, OKAY?
YOU'RE COMPROMISING THE DIGNITY OF THIS COMPLEX.

BLUSH
UH...
da-doom
Oh gosh. Here it is again, darn it!
da-doom
NOTHING! REALLY!
Stop it! Stop throbbing on me!
?
WHAT?
GROK
WAAH!
SPLAT
GYARGH!
disgusted
...
PA-THETIC...
TALK ABOUT HUMILIA-TINGLY LAME.
HOW ABOUT HELPING ME UP...?

WHAT'S THIS?
HUH ...?
Looks at people's stuff without asking
NO!
"CUTIE-PIES IN LOVE" ...?
GOOD LORD!
WHO'D WANNA SEE SOMETHING LIKE THAT?
What a cornball title
miff
I MEAN, JEEZ, YOU'D HAVE TO BE BRAIN-DEAD OR SOMETHING TO WANNA SEE THIS.
What a total jerk.
DON'T YOU HAVE ANY FRIENDS?
WHY'S IT ALWAYS YOUR BROTHER?
WHO SAID YOU COULD OPEN THAT? GIVE IT BACK!
NO... YOU DON'T... I'M GONNA GO SEE IT WITH MY BROTHER, SO THERE...
PWIK
Not listening.
Maybe I have a heart condition or something.

IT'S TWISTED, OKAY?
I got it...
YOU GUYS ARE TOO CLOSE FOR COMFORT!
I MEAN... WHAT WAS THAT LAST NIGHT, ANYWAY? ALL THAT HOOCHY-KOOCHY LOVEY-DOVEY...
It's because he's always scared me. I'm not used to him...
So I get nervous, and my heart starts pounding. That's gotta be it.
HOOCHY-KOOCHY LOVEY-DOVEY...
Still at it
Not listening
So if I spend more time with him (gulp)...
I'll get used to him. And then let's see...
...if this heart-throbbing still happens.
...UH... UMMM...
WOULD... YOU... UH...
GO... TO...THAT MOVIE WITH ME?!

Omigod.
I... OH... IT'S...
Totally embarrassing !!
JUST TO SEE IF... NO NO NO! UMM...
This is so...
TOMOR-ROW'S... SATURDAY... SO...
IF... YOU, UH...
... DON'T... HAVE ANY PLANS...
phlap

JAB
NOON TOMORROW. BY THE FOUNTAIN AT THE EAST EXIT OF THE STATION.
YOU BETTER NOT BE LATE!
LUCKY FOR YOU I JUST HAPPEN TO BE FREE TOMORROW.
SO I'LL DO YOU A FAVOR AND GO...
THOUGH I KNOW I'M GONNA BE BORED TO DEATH.
WHAT A TOTAL JERK!
...I DEFINITELY ...
...AM NOT IN LOVE WITH HIM...
01
TACHIBAN
SLAM

WELCOME HOME, YOUNG MASTER RYOKI.
MARIKO-SAN.
HOW'VE YOU BEEN?
I DIDN'T KNOW YOU'D BE HERE.
Smile
RYOKI DEAR, I'M SURE I MENTIONED SHE WAS COMING.
YOU KNOW I'M OFF TO ASHIYA TOMORROW TO VISIT YOUR GRANDPARENTS. I RECALL SAYING WE'D HAVE THE MAID HERE WHILE I'M GONE.
HOO HOO HOO
DON'T YOU REMEMBER?
I'D BE PERFECTLY FINE ON MY OWN...
I MUST DISAGREE! YOU HAVE THOSE IMPORTANT NATIONWIDE PRACTICE EXAMINATIONS TOMORROW AND SUNDAY.
YOUR TEACHERS AND I EXPECT YOU TO MAINTAIN YOUR TOP RANKING. YOU CERTAINLY CAN'T BE EXPECTED TO LOOK AFTER YOURSELF AT A TIME LIKE THIS!
...OH. I'M SORRY, BUT I WON'T BE TAKING TOMORROW'S PRACTICE EXAM AFTER ALL.
RYO --
SOME-THING HAS COME UP. DON'T WORRY, MOTHER. I'LL DO WELL ON SUNDAY'S EXAM.
KA- CHAK

RYOKI DEAR!
RAP RAP RAP
LET ME IN, RYOKI!!
WHUMP
FFF
HA HA HA HA HA HA HA HA HA
WHAT ON EARTH...
WHAT HAS GOTTEN INTO HIM?!

I'm already regretting this.
shwup
I shouldn't have asked him...
SHWUP
shwup
That was really hasty...
No! This is good!
Now I'll know it was just nervousness!
KA-CHAK
I'm definitely NOT in love with him.
AAAARGH. HELP ME, HATSUMI... THIS IS KILLING ME.
LEMME WASH MY FACE, I NEED TO WAKE UP.
YOU WON'T BELIEVE HOW MANY PAGES THE ENGLISH TEST COVERS.
YOUR MID-TERMS START NEXT WEEK?
SPLASH
YEAH ... OH! HEY...
WHERE'S SHINOGU? IT'S LATE. ISN'T HE HOME YET?
Shinogu...

IT SEEMS TO ME . . .
...THAT YOU'RE FALLING IN LOVE ...
...WITH RYOKI, HATSUMI.
This is not true. I am not in love with Ryoki.
I don't WANT to be in love with him.

I REALLY DON'T WANT TO...
HM ...?
...BACK HERE. SHINOGU!
SHINOGU!
Huh ...?
What is it ...?
MOM, I ALREADY SIGNED THE LEASE.
Shinogu's home... Guess I fell asleep...
KA-CHAK
BUT YOU CAN'T JUST MOVE OUT--
I'M SORRY, MOM, BUT TONIGHT'S THE ONLY TIME I CAN USE THE CAR.
PLUS...

I ALREADY GOT DAD'S PERMISSION, WAY BACK. HE SAID I COULD MOVE OUT OF THE HOUSE...
...IF I SAVED UP ENOUGH MONEY TO PAY THE RENT MYSELF.
SHINOGU! YOU'RE MOVING OUT?!
OH... I'M SORRY. DID WE WAKE YOU UP?
I SHOULD'VE KEPT MY VOICE DOWN, BUT WHEN HE SUDDENLY TELLS ME...

...I'M MOVING IN WITH A FRIEND.
A REALLY GOOD PLACE CAME UP, SO WE GRABBED IT.
AND THEN A FRIEND AT WORK SAID I COULD USE HIS VAN TONIGHT, SO...
AND IT ISN'T SO SUDDEN, MOM.
YOU KNEW I WANTED TO MOVE OUT. I TOLD YOU.
BUT LEAVING IN THE MIDDLE OF THE NIGHT, LIKE A FUGITIVE...!
I... NEVER HEARD ABOUT IT.
DON'T WORRY, MOM! THE COPS AREN'T AFTER ME!
LOOK, I'M ONLY TAKING THE STUFF I NEED RIGHT AWAY. I'LL BE BACK TO PACK UP MY OTHER STUFF.
HA HA HA HA!
BUT... SHINOGU! JUST HOLD ON!
IT'S ALL RIGHT, HATSUMI.
I'LL BE COMING EVERY WEDNESDAY FOR THE TUTORING SESSIONS.
SHINOGU!

THIS IS WHY...
...I WAS WORKING SO MANY JOBS. SO I COULD SAVE UP THE MONEY TO MOVE OUT.
...I WAS KEEPING IT A SECRET.
I THOUGHT I WOULD SURPRISE YOU.
COME ON, HATSUMI. TELL ME YOU'RE PROUD OF ME.
BUT... YOU NEVER TOLD ME. I DIDN'T... KNOW.
I DON'T LIKE THIS KIND OF SURPRISE!
SHH! KEEP YOUR VOICE DOWN, HATSUMI.
AKANE JUST WENT TO SLEEP A LITTLE WHILE AGO.

WELL. IF WE CARRY ON WE'LL WAKE UP OUR NEIGHBORS... I SUPPOSE I'LL HAVE TO LET YOU GO.
BUT I'M CALLING YOUR FATHER FIRST THING IN THE MORNING, IS THAT CLEAR?!
AND I'M SAYING HELLO TO YOUR FRIEND AND THANKING HIM FOR HIS TROUBLE.
OH. OKAY. HE'S DOWN-STAIRS...
MOM!
BAM
...
WHERE... ARE YOU GOING...?
SOMEWHERE CLOSE BY? IT ISN'T FAR AWAY, IS IT?
IT'S RIGHT BY MY SCHOOL.
NISHI-KOKUBUNJI, ON THE CHUO LINE. IT'S FAR. REALLY FAR.
SO... I GUESS WE WON'T BE SEEING SO MUCH OF EACH OTHER.

BYE!
TAKE CARE!
BAM
302
NARITA
...BUT... WHY...?
WHY SO SUDDEN ...?

...
SO...
...BECAUSE... I CAN'T...
...KEEP MY PROMISE... TO GOD...
I CAN'T BE WITH YOU ANY-MORE.

WHAAT?! SHINOGU MOVED OUT?!
NO WAY! IS THAT FOR REAL?!
LUCKY DUCK!! I AM SO JEALOUS!
HOW COOL! NOW HE GETS TO DO WHATEVER HE WANTS. GOSH...
I CAN'T **WAIT** TO GROW UP SO I CAN MOVE OUT, TOO!
BUT... AREN'T YOU GOING TO MISS HIM? I HATE THIS...I WISH HE'D COME BACK.
...YOU AND SHINOGU ARE WAY TOO CLOSE, I SWEAR.
YOU SHOULD JUST GET OVER IT AND START GOING OUT WITH RYOKI.
WHAT ARE YOU...!

OMIGOD! OMIGOD! OMIGOD!
WHAT?!
WHAT IS IT?!
I totally forgot.
And I'm the one who asked **him** out.
NOON TOMORROW.
YOU BETTER NOT BE LATE!
Guess I have to go.
But now I **really** don't feel like it.
Shinogu was definitely acting strange.
Something's the matter.
kyuween
I mean...

glance
glance
glance
...SHE'S LATE.*
*They're meeting at 12:00

SHE'S TOTALLY LATE.
GULP
I HEARD. EVERY-BODY'S TALKING ABOUT IT.
SHINOGU MOVED OUT LAST NIGHT?

HE FINALLY HAD TO GO, HUH?
POOR GUY.
GRIP

WHAT DO YOU MEAN, "POOR GUY"?
WHY'D YOU SAY THAT?
YOU KNOW SOMETHING ABOUT SHINOGU, AZUSA?!
...SO IT'S TRUE.
YOU REALLY DON'T KNOW.
KNOW WHAT?! AND HOW COME ***YOU*** KNOW ABOUT IT?
DON'T... TELL...ME... IT'S GOT SOMETHING TO DO WITH MY FATHER...?
I'LL TELL YOU IF YOU DON'T CRY.

MAYBE HE FELT LIKE HE DOESN'T BELONG.
IN YOUR FAMILY, I MEAN. **SHINOGU... ISN'T YOUR PARENTS' KID.**
gimmick

Chapter 21

ANOTHER 10 MINUTES GONE BY...

SHINOGU ISN'T YOUR PARENTS' KID.

SHINOGU
...
...
ISN'T
...
...YOUR PARENTS' KID.
...
YOU'RE... LYING...
YOU THINK I'LL FALL FOR ANYTHING, DON'T YOU, AZUSA?
BUT I'M NOT BELIEVING YOU THIS TIME, NO WAY.
AS IF...THAT'S JUST WAY TOO OUT THERE.

IF IT WAS JUST WHAT YOU SAID ABOUT MY DAD, THEN MAYBE.
BUT I DON'T EVEN KNOW FOR SURE IF ***THAT'S*** TRUE OR NOT.
SO DON'T GO AROUND SAYING WEIRD STUFF ABOUT MY BROTHER.
BYE. I HAVE TO GO...
SHINOGU KNOWS.
BUT I GUESS HE WANTED TO KEEP IT A SECRET FROM YOU.
THAT'S WHY HE DIDN'T GET IN MY WAY THAT TIME.
HE KNEW I WAS DUPING YOU. THAT I WAS UP TO SOME-THING...
BUT HE DIDN'T STOP ME, CUZ HE DIDN'T WANT ME TO BLAB.

...I'M SORRY.
Oh my god. That's right.
SEE, I KNEW ...
I KNEW THAT... AND I COULDN'T PROTECT YOU.
I'M SORRY, HATSUMI...
...THAT AZUSA WAS PLANNING SOMETHING THAT MIGHT HURT YOU...
...WANNA HEAR MORE?
That's what he ...

IF YOU DON'T MIND TALKING ABOUT IT RIGHT HERE IN THE MIDDLE OF THE WHOLE COMPLEX...
I CAN TELL YOU EVERYTHING I KNOW.
YIKES
YOU SURE YOU WANT ME TO TELL YOU RIGHT HERE?

...BUT OH, THAT'S RIGHT.
YOU AREN'T GONNA BELIEVE ME ANYWAY, ARE YOU? CUZ I'M SUCH A BIG LIAR.
SO LET'S JUST FORGET IT.
W... WAIT!
DIDN'T YOU SAY YOU HAVE TO GO?

OH...

That's... right. I do.

Ryoki will kill me if I keep him waiting.

But...
But I...
BRRRRING BRRRRING BRRRR-
I GOT IT, I GOT IT!
PATTA PATTA PATTA
BRRRING
HELLOOO! NARITA RESI--
CHAK
YOU'RE LATE, YOU STUPID DITZ! WHAT'RE YOU DOING?!
WONK
EEK!
LOOK, YOU'RE THE ONE WHO ASKED ME OUT, OKAY?!

THAT MEANS YOU'RE SUPPOSED TO GET HERE HALF AN HOUR AHEAD OF TIME AND WAIT FOR ME!
AND NOW IT'S FIVE TO TWELVE AND WHERE THE HELL ARE YOU? AT HOME! GET YOUR ASS DOWN HERE, YOU **DOPE!**
I'M COUNTING TO TEN, ALL RIGHT? IF YOU AREN'T HERE BY --
WHOA, WHOA, WHOA! HOLD ON! RYOKI-KUN...? IS THAT YOU?
THIS IS AKANE. AKANE! THIS ISN'T HATSUMI, IT'S HER...
...OH... JUNIOR...
DON'T CALL ME "JUNIOR"!
IF YOU WANT HATSUMI, SHE LEFT A WHILE AGO.
HEY... SO SHE HAD A DATE? WITH YOU? HMMM...
WHO KNEW? HERE SHE WAS ALL ACTING LIKE SHE'S IN SHOCK OVER SHINOGU, AND THEN SHE GOES OFF ON A DATE? I'M SO SURE!
SHINO-GU...?
DID SOME-THING HAPPEN TO HIM?

Oh no! He's already there!! (Three minutes early.)
UH... UMM!
HUFF
HUFF
I, UH... I'M...
FWAP
...SORRY.
I'M REALLY SORRY, BUT...
I... CAN'T, UM...
...GO, TODAY...
CUZ, UMM...

grip
HEY...
COME ON. WE'RE CATCHING THE TRAIN AT TEN PAST.
WHAT? BUT... WAIT! I CAN'T...
GLARE
YOU AREN'T ABOUT TO SAY SOMETHING **DUMB** LIKE...
...YOUR BROTHER MOVED OUT AND YOU'RE TOO UPSET TO GO, ARE YOU?!
HOW DID YOU KNOW...? ABOUT...
I JUST CALLED YOUR HOUSE, AND YOUR SISTER TOLD ME ABOUT IT.
WHAT?!

Oh no. That means Akane knows about...
LOOK, IN CASE YOU FORGOT...
YOU'RE THE ONE WHO ASKED ME TO COME.
I KNOW. BUT YESTERDAY...
I DIDN'T KNOW ABOUT SHINOGU YET, SO...
THAT'S NONE OF MY BUSINESS.
LOOK, I PUT ASIDE A BIG PRAC--
ka-chank
...UH, THAT IS...
I PUT ASIDE VALUABLE TIME FOR YOU.
SO BE MORE FUN.
1
Easy for him to say.
How am I supposed to have fun?
All I want to do is go home...
...and get to the bottom of this.

Ask Mom or Shinogu to find out if it's true.
YOU BETTER NOT TRY TO RUN OFF RIGHT AFTER, OKAY? WE'RE STAYING OUT.
TILL PRETTY LATE. LIKE, AFTER...
...DARK.
But how would I ask? What do I say?
I MEAN, YOU ASKED ME OUT!
HEH HEH
We're not brother and sister.
Or figure out why Azusa knows in the first place.
HEY, SINCE I'M DOING YOU THE FAVOR OF SEEING THAT LAME MOVIE...
It has to be a lie...
HEY, YOU LISTENING TO ME?
HEY!
IT HAS TO BE!

I...
...JUST HEARD THAT SHINOGU...
PWIK
... MIGHT...
...MIGHT NOT... BE...
What are you doing?! Don't be stupid!
Don't talk to **him** about it.
...MY REAL BROTHER...
...THAT MAYBE HE'S ADOPTED, AND...
But I just can't deal with this alone. I don't know what to do.
Maybe ...
... Ryoki can help me.
I JUST CAN'T BELIEVE IT, BUT STILL...

hotgimmick

Just maybe ...
...if I talk to him, he might ...
I JUST DON'T KNOW WHAT TO...
SO WHAT?

WHAT'S IT GOT TO DO WITH ME?
I MEAN...
SO YOUR BROTHER MOVED OUT OF THE HOUSE.
SO HE MIGHT NOT REALLY BE YOUR BROTHER. IS THAT ANY CONCERN OF MINE?
I DON'T THINK SO.
PISSES ME OFF. ASK ME OUT...
AND THEN ALL YOU DO IS TALK ABOUT YOUR BROTHER.
AND MOPE AROUND. JEEZ.
YOU REALLY PISS ME OFF.
I'M GOING HOME.

WHAT?!
YOU'RE KIDDING! HANG ON...
TRRRRRR
SHWOOOOO
PHOOSH
TEE HEE
TEE HEE
TEE HEE

TEE HEE
DID HE JUST DUMP HER?
TEE HEE
HOW EMBAR-RASSING! I WOULD DIE IF THAT WAS ME.
SNIFF
I hate him.
I do.
He obviously doesn't care about me at all.

bip
bip
bip
bip
......
plop
rustle
GLASSES BACK ON
not particularly significant, actually...
CHAK

705
ODAGI
REPORT OF INVESTIGATION INTO TORU NARITA
Kyowa Investigations, Head Office
Kanda 0-01 Chiyoda-ku, Toky
0120-000-0120
IF I KEEP STIRRING THINGS UP...
...AND MAKE A REAL MESS OF THIS FAMILY...
WILL THAT SCUMBAG... FINALLY APOLOGIZE FOR WHAT HE DID?
MOM...
TUMP
...UNTIL THEN...

...I WONDER HOW MUCH MORE I'M GONNA HURT HER?
HATSUMI...
I'M HOME ...
HEEEY!
HATSUUU-MEEE! ♡
HEY HEY HEY! WHY DIDN'T YOU TELL ME? THAT --
WAITA-MINIT...
VWIP
WHAT ABOUT YOUR DATE?!
HOW COME YOU'RE HOME ALREADY?
WHAT HAP-PENED TO YOUR DATE?
IT WASN'T A DATE!

HEY! WHEN DID MOM SAY SHE WAS COMING HOME TODAY?
HM? OH...
SHE SAID SHE'D BE LATE TODAY.
THERE'S A PARTY AFTER WORK FOR SOMEONE WHO'S LEAVING.
CHILD-CARE INCLUDED.

...OH... SHE'LL BE LATE...
Well... I wouldn't even know how to ask her, anyway.
...
HATSUMI...? YOU OKAY?

HEY... I'M HERE IF YOU WANT TO TALK.
What? Akane knows?!
OH. AKANE...

RYOKI DUMPED YOU, DIDN'T HE?!!
I KNEW THIS WOULD HAPPEN!
I MEAN, YOU'RE JUST NOT IN HIS LEAGUE. I GUESS HE CAME TO HIS SENSES OR SOME-THING.
BUT DON'T EVEN THINK ABOUT SUBARU, OKAY?!
HE'S NOT YOUR TYPE AT ALL!
...THANKS A LOT.
DON'T YOU HAVE TO STUDY FOR THOSE MIDTERMS ...?
BUT ...
OH, SPEAKING OF RYOKI, HE --
...CALLED A LITTLE WHILE AGO...
BAM
I don't want to hear about Ryoki.
What really makes me mad...
...is that I was dumb enough to turn to him for help.
Hm?

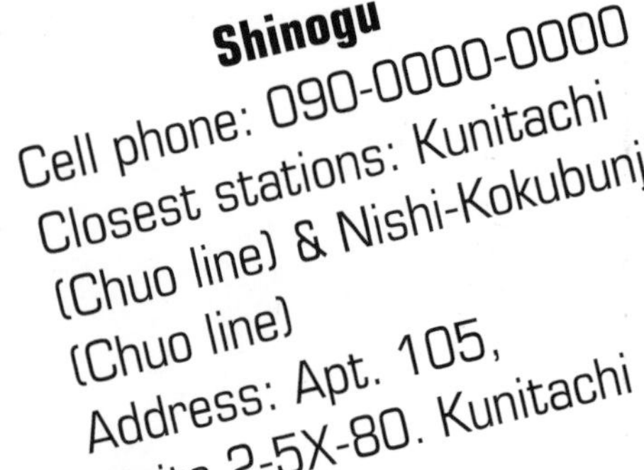

Shinogu

Cell phone: 090-0000-0000
Closest stations: Kunitachi
(Chuo line) & Nishi-Kokubunji
(Chuo line)
Address: Apt. 105,
Naito 2-5X-80. Kunitachi

That's right.
Forget about Mom.
I'll just go and ask Shinogu directly.
ka-chak
For all I know...

He'll just laugh and tell me Azusa's playing games with me.
HUH? YOU'RE GOING OUT AGAIN?
YEAH.
After all, there's no point in sitting here wondering.
OH, YEAH. I FORGOT TO TELL YOU EARLIER, BUT --
IF IT'S ABOUT RYOKI, I DON'T WANNA HEAR IT.
NO. IT'S DAD. HE'S COMING HOME TOMORROW.
HE CALLED HERE EARLIER.
REMEMBER MOM CALLED HIM THIS MORNING ABOUT SHINOGU MOVING OUT?
DAD...
HE SAID TO TELL SHINOGU TO BE HERE, CUZ HE WANTS TO SIT DOWN AND TALK.

All right! Cool! Bring him on!
This is perfect. I'm going to ask him straight out about everything.
And let's clear up the whole Azusa deal while we're at it!!
HA-TSUMI!
SUBA-RU.
GLAD I RAN INTO YOU. HEY...
ASAHI WANTS TO PRACTICE HAIRDOS ON YOU TONIGHT. YOU FREE?
SORRY... I'M... GOING OUT RIGHT NOW.
AKANE'S HOME, THOUGH.
YIKES!
SHE IS?!
...OH, BUT... SHE'S STUDYING FOR HER MIDTERMS RIGHT NOW. THEY START MONDAY, SO...
FORGET IT!! SHE DOESN'T HAVE THE TIME, FOR SURE!!

GOSH, EVERY-ONE'S BUSY THIS WEEKEND, HUH?
RYO HAS THOSE BIG PRACTICE EXAMS TODAY AND TOMORROW ...
...HUH ...?
RYOKI ...?
...HAD A PRACTICE EXAM...? TODAY...?
YEAH.
SOME BIG NATIONAL ONE. HE WAS STUDYING PRETTY HARD, FOR A CHANGE.
I JUST HAPPEN TO BE FREE TOMORROW.
SO I'LL DO YOU A FAVOR AND GO.

...?
HATSUMI?
NO WAY.
He didn't have to skip an important exam.
Then why didn't he just say so? We could've gone to a movie another time.
All he had to do was tell me he's busy.
KA-THUNK
KA-THUNK

Omigod.
He did that for me?
KYUWEEN
KYEEEEEE
No.
Come on.
I can't think about stuff like that right now.
くにたち
国立
Kunitachi
And what about the way he just left me on the train?!
I thought I hated him so much.
WHUMP
OH. EXCUSE ME...

How come ...
DA-DOOM!
... HE'S here ?

SIGH
...WHY THE HELL...
...ARE *YOU* HERE?
WHAT?!

JEEZ... WHAT, YOU CAN'T STAY AWAY FROM YOUR BROTHER FOR ONE DAY...?
THAT'S NOT...
PISSES ME OFF! Fine, whatever!
SO SHOW ME THE WAY. TO YOUR BROTHER'S.
BUT I...IT'S MY FIRST TIME, SO...
I'M NOT REALLY SURE...
WHAT?! JEEZ, YOU'RE USE-LESS!
GUESS WE HAVE TO WALK AROUND LOOKING AT HOUSE NUMBERS.
SHE SAID TO GO OUT THE WEST EXIT AND...
RYOKI...? WHY ARE YOU HERE...?
YOU... DIDN'T COME...
...ALL THIS WAY... TO SEE MY BROTHER... DID YOU?
WHY *ELSE* WOULD I COME THE HELL OUT HERE?!

BUT... WHY?
I GOT HIS CELL PHONE NUMBER FROM YOUR SISTER AND CALLED HIM, BUT HE DIDN'T ANSWER.
SO I THOUGHT IT'D BE FASTER TO JUST COME OUT HERE AND SEE HIM.
CUZ *NOW* I HAVE ALL THIS TIME TO KILL!
OH...
UMM... I...
YOU KNOW, EARLIER...?
BASI-CALLY...
I JUST NEED TO SEE YOUR BROTHER TO GIVE HIM A PIECE OF MY MIND!
YOUR FAMILY'S GOT WAY TOO MANY PROBLEMS!
ZAP

FIRST IT'S YOUR DAD AND WAS HE FOOLING AROUND OR NOT.
NOW IT'S YOUR BROTHER MOVING OUT AND IS HE REALLY YOUR BROTHER OR NOT.
I MEAN, IT'S JUST ONE THING AFTER ANOTHER.
THIS IS WHY...
...YOU CAN'T FOCUS ALL YOUR ATTENTION ON ME.
PISSES ME OFF.
YOU'RE TOO STUPID TO THINK ABOUT MORE THAN ONE THING AT A TIME!
SO I FIGURED, I'D GET YOUR BROTHER TO TALK...
...AND THE WHOLE MYSTERY'S SOLVED, RIGHT?

HEY, WE'VE BEEN WALKING A LONG TIME.
IT SHOULD BE AROUND HERE...
IS IT A BIG BUILDING? SMALL?
WHAT'S IT CALLED AGAIN?
HEY! HA-TSUMI?
...?
WHAT'RE YOU DOING?
SOME-TIMES...
IT'S HARD TO TELL WHETHER YOU'RE BEING...
...MEAN OR NICE...
HUH?

YOU'RE MEAN, AND THEN YOU'RE NICE...
I DON'T KNOW HOW I'M SUP-POSED TO TAKE IT...
WHAT?
WHEN WAS I EVER NICE TO YOU?
YOU'RE NICE... SOME-TIMES.
LIKE NOW.
HUH?
CUZ I CAME TO GIVE YOUR BROTHER THE THIRD DEGREE?
AND YOU HELPED US THAT TIME...WHEN EVERYONE WAS IGNORING US.
BUT THAT WAS JUST TO MAKE YOU OWE ME, SO I COULD USE THAT TO...
AND AFTER WE WENT TO AZUSA'S, YOU PATTED ME ON THE HEAD AND SAID I DID OKAY.
THAT WAS ONLY BECAUSE YOU DIDN'T FUSS OVER HIM.
The idea
Attagirl! All right! Good girl!
WOOF!
...AND THEN TODAY...
YOU SKIPPED THAT PRACTICE EXAM...TO GO OUT WITH ME.

...
IT WASN'T...A BIG-DEAL EXAM OR ANYTHING... IT REALLY... WAS NO BIG DEAL...
DAMN IT! BET IT WAS SUBARU...
I DIDN'T BAIL ON IT FOR YOUR SAKE OR ANYTHING, IT JUST...IT DOESN'T MATTER...
BUT...!
DA-DOOM
MY HEART STARTS THROBBING.
DA-DOOM

I CAN'T REALLY EXPLAIN IT...
YOU... SCARE ME, AND...
I... THOUGHT I HATED YOU, BUT...
DA-DOOM
WHEN YOU DO THINGS LIKE THAT, I...
MY HEART STARTS THROBBING, AND I...
DA-DOOM
...JUST DON'T KNOW WHAT TO...
DA-DOOM

...STARTS THROBBING ?
OVER ME?

...
OH MY GOD.
BWOFF!
I PRACTICALLY TOLD HIM I'M IN LOVE WITH HIM...!
UH... UMM... ERRR... UMM... ERR...
RIGHT! WE WERE LOOKING FOR SHINOGU'S NEW PLACE!
WHAT WAS THE NUMBER AGAIN?
HOLD IT.
YIKES!

DA-DOO
DA-DOOM
DA-DOOM
DA-DOOM
DA-DOOM

DA-DOOM
DA-DOOM
DA-DOOM
STROKE
DA-DOOM
STROKE
DON'T ...
DON'T TEASE ...

DA-DOOM
DA-DOOM
DA-DOOM

DA-DOOOM
...NOW LOOK WHAT YOU DID.
DA-DOOOM
IT MUST BE CONTAGIOUS.
DA-DOOOM

DA-DOOOM
DA-DOOOM
...HATSUMI.
THIS IS MY FINAL OFFER.
DA-DOOOM
RIGHT NOW, I'M STILL WILLING...
...TO LET YOU BE MY GIRLFRIEND.

WHAT DO YOU SAY?
DA-DOOM

...OH...
SHINOGU...

Chapter 22

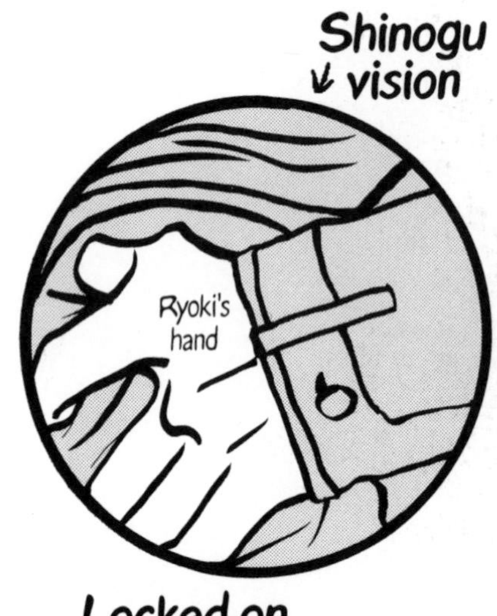
Shinogu
vision
Ryoki's
hand
Locked on
Hatsumi!

...OH...

SHINOGU
...

Umm...
If you want to know what all this means...
Shinogu suddenly moved out of the house.
TAKE CARE.
SHINOGU NARITA (big brother)
AKANE NARITA (little sister)
Which came as a pretty big shock to me. So I was freaking out about that, when...
YOU AND SHINOGU ARE WAY TOO CLOSE, I SWEAR!
Azusa says ...
MAYBE HE FELT LIKE HE DOESN'T BELONG.
IN YOUR FAMILY, I MEAN. SHINOGU... ISN'T YOUR PARENTS' KID.
Childhood friend # 1: AZUSA ODAGIRI

At the station near Shinogu's apartment...
Royal cape
I bumped into Ryoki, who had just ditched me earlier in a total huff.
Childhood friend #2:
RYOKI TACHIBANA
I know that's gotta be a lie.
But I wanted to know why Shinogu moved out all of a sudden like that, so...
I went to see him at his new place.
When I realized...
IT MUST BE CONTA-GIOUS.
...that maybe ...
... Ryoki was there because he cares about me...
It just ...
RIGHT NOW, I'M STILL WILLING...
...TO LET YOU BE MY GIRL-FRIEND.
WHAT DO YOU SAY?
...made my heart start beating so fast.
I hardly knew what to do...

And that's when ...
...my brother came along.
SCHOOL CROSSING
OH, GOOD!
WE WERE JUST LOOKING FOR YOUR NEW PLACE...
PHEW

I, UMM...
I'M SAVED.
I WANTED TO TALK TO YOU ABOUT SOMETHING.
Right now.
TALK TO ME...?
I need to talk to Shinogu. That's why I'm here.
And anyway...
There's no way I could ever become Ryoki's girlfriend!
I mean, no way! There is no way!!
Even so...

I was about to say...
... Yes ...
...to him just now. I really was.
YEAH, I KNOW. HE CALLED ME.
UM. UH...
DAD'S COMING HOME TOMORROW... SO...
I'LL BE COMING HOME TONIGHT.
MIGHT BE KINDA LATE, CUZ I'M HELPING MY ROOMMATE MOVE HIS STUFF IN HERE FIRST.

OH YEAH... DO I KNOW HIM? YOUR NEW ROOM-MATE.
IS HE A FRIEND FROM SCHOOL? OH, IS IT THAT GUY WHO...
IT'S A GUY I WORK WITH. YOU DON'T KNOW HIM.
OH. OH, WELL...
He seems like he's in a bad mood.
Hey. Is he...
...mad at me ...?
Oh, I know. Maybe it's because I just suddenly showed up (with Ryoki, to boot).
Now what? That makes it hard to bring it up.
GLUG GLUG
...SO?
IS THAT IT?
YOU DONE ?
URGH!
NO... UH...
IT'S ...
AZUSA SAID...

...THAT YOU AREN'T REALLY YOUR PARENTS' KID. HE TOLD HATSUMI...
...THAT MAYBE THAT'S THE REASON YOU MOVED OUT.
BECAUSE YOU DIDN'T FEEL LIKE YOU BELONGED THERE.
RYO --
SO, THAT'S WHY SHE'S HERE.
RYOKI!
SHE WANTED TO ASK YOU IF THAT'S TRUE OR NOT.

THAT IS WHY YOU'RE HERE, RIGHT?!
UH...
WELL, COME ON. RIGHT?
I KNEW YOU WOULDN'T BE ABLE TO ASK HIM YOURSELF. BE GRATE-FUL I'M HERE!
NO...
NO, THAT'S ...
SO JUST TELL HER WHETHER IT'S TRUE OR NOT, WHAT AZUSA SAID.
BECAUSE IF IT IS, WELL, MAYBE HATSUMI WILL FINALLY GROW UP...
...AND LEARN TO LIVE WITHOUT YOU!
RIGHT? HEY, HATSUMI. RIGHT?
NO, IT ISN'T.

YOU'RE MY BROTHER.
NO MATTER WHAT HAPPENS, YOU'LL ALWAYS BE MY BROTHER!
I DON'T CARE WHAT AZUSA SAYS.
IT DOESN'T MATTER.
YOU'LL ALWAYS BE MY BROTHER, SHINOGU!!

HATSUMI...
SO... WHAT I WANTED TO ASK YOU...
...WASN'T THAT AT ALL. THE REASON I CAME HERE TO TALK TO YOU IS...
WELL, I'VE BEEN WONDERING WHY AZUSA SAID THAT TO ME.
AND I THOUGHT IT MIGHT BE CONNECTED TO THAT THING ABOUT DAD AND AZUSA'S MOM HAVING AN AFFAIR.
I THOUGHT MAYBE YOU MIGHT ACTUALLY KNOW THE TRUTH ABOUT THAT WHOLE STORY...

THAT MAYBE DAD'S SECRET HAS BEEN WEIGHING YOU DOWN, BECAUSE YOU'RE THE ONLY ONE WHO KNOWS.
AND IF THAT'S WHY...
IF THAT'S WHY YOU MOVED OUT, BECAUSE YOU COULDN'T TAKE IT, I...
HATSUMI.
HATSUMI, IT'S ALL RIGHT. THAT'S NOT IT.
THAT ISN'T WHY I MOVED OUT. REALLY.
HONEST.

I JUST WANTED TO MOVE OUT, THAT'S ALL.
...YOU KNOW, BE ON MY OWN.
I MEAN, HOW LONG AM I SUPPOSED TO LIVE AT HOME, HUH? I'M ALL GROWN UP, RIGHT?
BUT!
...I ADMIT ...
THAT I WAS LYING TO YOU... ABOUT...
DAD... FOOLING AROUND...
YOU WERE REALLY SMALL AT THE TIME, SO YOU PROBABLY DON'T REMEMBER, BUT...
THERE WAS A TIME...
...WHEN MOM AND DAD WERE FIGHTING A LOT ABOUT STUFF LIKE THAT.
BUT I GUESS THE WHOLE THING WAS RESOLVED BEFORE IT TURNED INTO A BIG DEAL ABOUT WHO THE WOMAN WAS.
AND HEY, MOM AND DAD ARE STILL MARRIED, RIGHT? AND HIKARU WAS BORN AFTER ALL THAT.
SO I JUST DIDN'T WANT TO RAKE UP THE PAST AGAIN, YOU KNOW?

BUT... IT WASN'T THAT SIMPLE.
AZUSA'S REALLY HURT BECAUSE OF THIS.
HE TOTALLY HATES DAD FOR WHAT HAPPENED. HE HATES OUR WHOLE FAMILY.
I'LL TRY TO BRING THAT UP TOMORROW, WHEN I TALK TO DAD.
WITH AZUSA THERE, IF POSSIBLE. THE THREE OF US'LL TALK.
SO DON'T ***YOU*** LET THIS STUFF WEIGH YOU DOWN, EITHER.
I'M HERE FOR YOU, OKAY?
...I ***AM*** YOUR BROTHER, AFTER ALL.

OKAY...
SCOWL
SO THAT'S SET-TLED!
LET'S GO!
HUH?! HANG ON, RYOKI...
DING DONG
YOO-HOO, NARITA! I'M HERE!
OH. Y'ALL GOT VISI-TORS?

UH... YEAH. MY SISTER AND... WELL...
HEY, HATSUMI.
THIS IS MY ROOMMATE, KAZAMA.
OH! NICE TO MEET YOU!
BOY HOWDY, A GENU-INE KO-GAL! ♡ ♡
THIS IS, UH, A NICE PLACE YOU GUYS FOUND. I LIKE IT A LOT. UH...
HEY, DUDE, SHE'S A REAL CUTIE! ♡
I'M JUST GONNA PUT THIS STUFF AWAY REAL QUICK, SO WHY DON'T Y'ALL JUST SETTLE DOWN AND --
SHWA
NO THANK YOU.
WE WERE JUST LEAVING, ACTUALLY.
SORRY ABOUT THE INTRUSION. GOOD-BYE!
THUD THUD THUD THUD
UM, BYE, SHINOGU!
SEE YOU LATER! AT HOME, OKAY?
SLAM
WHAT THE HELL ...?
CHARMING L'IL BUGGER, AIN'T HE? GREAT GUY!
WHAT IS HE, YOUR SISTER'S FELLA?

...UH-HUH.
PROBAB-LY...
AT LEAST I THINK HE IS...
OW!
RYOKI! YOU'RE HURTING ME!

I KNOW HOW TO WALK, OKAY? YOU DON'T HAVE TO YANK ME ALONG LIKE THIS!
RYOKI!
...WHAT'S THE BIG HURRY, ANYWAY...? NOW THAT SHINOGU TOLD US ABOUT MY DAD...
I WANTED TO ASK HIM SOME QUES-TIONS.
PLUS, HIS ROOMMATE JUST GOT THERE. IT WAS A GREAT CHANCE TO GET ACQUAINTED WITH HIM. WHY COULDN'T WE...
Oh no! He's gonna hit me.
HYAAGH
Shut up and do as you're told!
BONK
Huh?

FINE.
SO GO BACK THERE, THEN.
WHA?
JUST GO BACK AND GET ALL LOVEY-DOVEY...
...WITH YOUR BROTHER AGAIN, LIKE YOU JUST WERE.
WHA--
I don't believe this! What is his problem?!
First he drags me out of there, and then this?!
AAAAARG

Fine! Forget about him!
I WILL go back. I'm going back. So there!!
But ...
Hey ...
I don't know.
He seems kinda... down. (He didn't even smack me).

I can't just ditch him and go back...
...when I see him walking away like that.
GOOD EVENING --
YO, AKANE!
YIPES!
HITTIN' THE BOOKS? HEARD YOU HAVE EXAMS NEXT WEEK.
WHAT'S UP, YOU NEEDED A LITTLE BREAK?

I NEED SOMETHING TO EAT. MY MOM'S COMING HOME LATE TONIGHT, AND...
IT'S HATSUMI'S TURN TO MAKE DINNER, BUT SHE WENT OUT AND NEVER CAME BACK, SO...
OH. THAT SUCKS...

I KNOW! COME EAT WITH US.
I'M MAKING CURRY. WHY DON'T YOU COME OVER?
WHAT ?!

REALLY? IS THAT COOL?
YEAH, TOTALLY.
OUR FOLKS ARE GONNA BE LATE TOO, SO WE CAN JUST KICK BACK.
WHISPER WHISPER
BRING ALONG SHINOGU'S NEW ADDRESS, OKAY? DEAL?
LET ME JUST GO PAY FOR THIS STUFF! ♡
WAIT FOR ME, OKAY?
SO THAT'S WHY SHE INVITED ME!

GLANCE

GREAT...

AFTER DINNER, YOU CAN HELP ME OUT WITH MY MATH.

WHAT?! NO I CAN'T!

I'M NO GOOD AT MATH, I SWEAR! GET RYO TO HELP YOU WITH THAT!

THIS IS JUNIOR HIGH STUFF. RYOKI'S SO FAR BEYOND IT.

YOU'D BE JUST PERFECT, SUBARU! ♡

GYAAAK

HIGASHI KOMAZAWA STATION

...UH... UMM ...
RYOKI ...?
THANKS FOR... UH... TODAY...
...
He hasn't said a word the whole way.
What's he so mad about, anyway? I can't figure it out.
Why did I follow him back here like this?
I should've just gone back to my brother's and come home later with **HIM**.
Plus, **I'm** the one who needs consolation here...
...after what I heard about Dad. That it's true he had an affair.
...YOU SATISFIED?
WITH JUST THAT.

MAYBE YOU KNOW A LITTLE MORE ABOUT YOUR DAD NOW, BUT...
YOUR BROTHER DIDN'T SAY ANYTHING ABOUT WHETHER HE'S ADOPTED OR NOT, DID HE?
THAT WASN'T CLEARED UP AT ALL.
Finally...
He says some-thing.
OH... WELL, THAT.
IT'S LIKE I SAID...AS FAR AS I'M CONCERNED, SHINOGU'S MY --
YEAH, YEAH. WHAT-EVER.

YOU DON'T WANT TO KNOW THE TRUTH, DO YOU?
BECAUSE YOU CAN'T STAND THE THOUGHT OF LOSING HIM.
WHAT ...?
...YOU KNOW WHAT I FEEL LIKE? A TOTAL CHUMP.
I'M SICK OF THIS.

GO AHEAD...

BE ALL LOVEY-DOVEY WITH YOUR BROTHER FOR THE REST OF YOUR LIFE.

AND STOP FOLLOWING ME AROUND!

BUT WE LIVE IN THE SAME BUILDING.

I HAVE TO FOLLOW YOU...

LOOK, IT'S A PAIN IF PEOPLE FROM THE COMPLEX SEE US TOGETHER. THAT'S WHY WE MET AT THE STATION TODAY.

KILL SOME TIME AND GO HOME LATER. BYE!

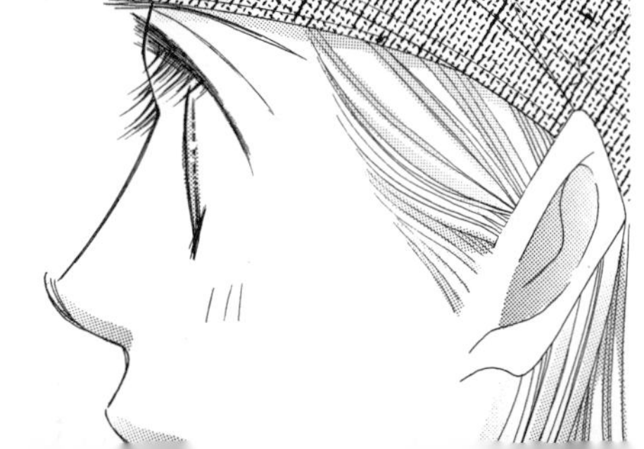

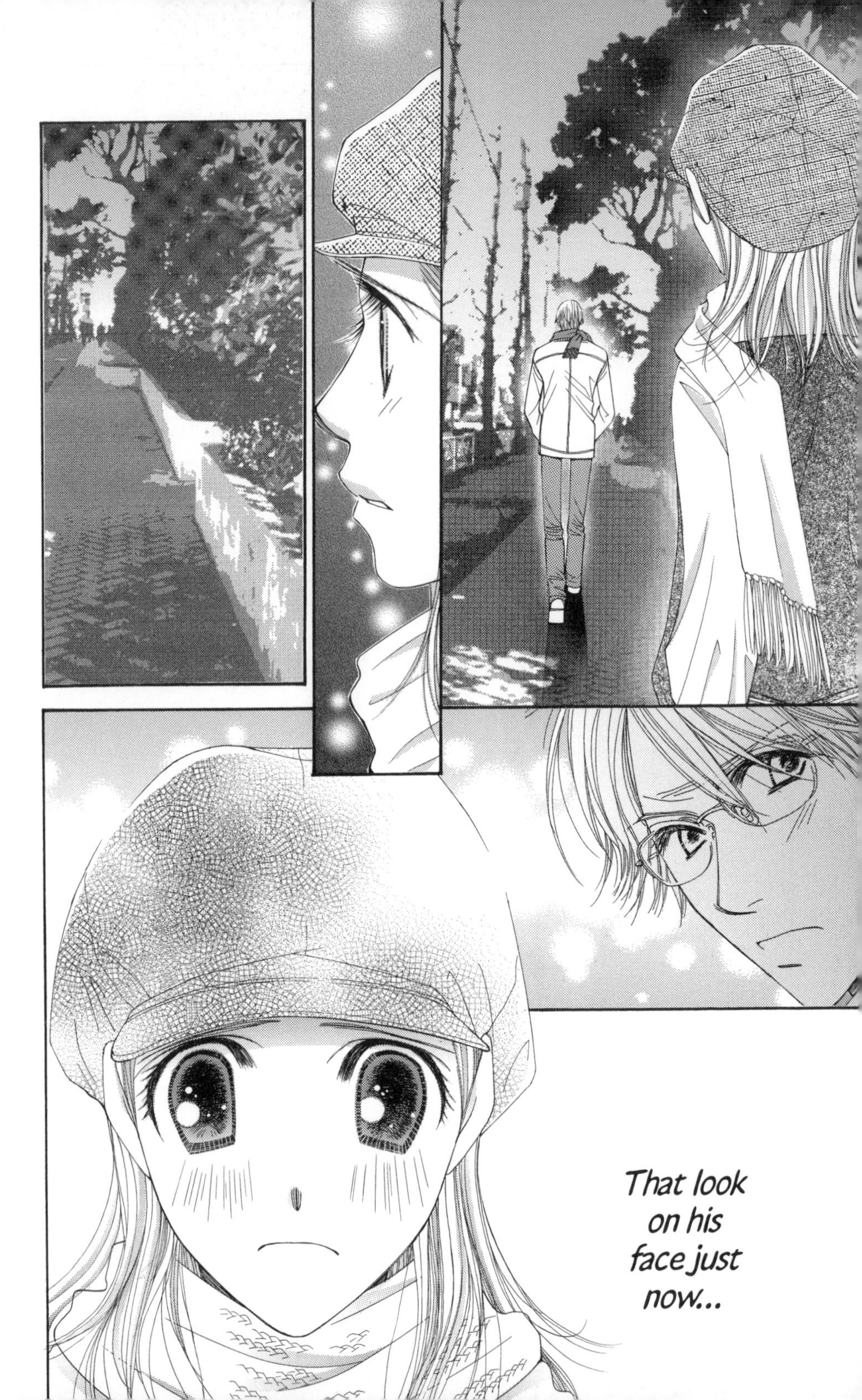
That look
on his
face just
now...

That wasn't anger, was it?
It was jealousy...
...I don't believe it.
Why get so bummed out over my brother?
I don't believe it.

OH, FORGET ABOUT HIM!
I HAVE OTHER THINGS TO THINK ABOUT. LIKE MAKING DINNER...
BUT HEY, WHERE'S AKANE? SHE ISN'T HOME?
I really don't have the time...
...to be worrying about Ryoki right now...
THAT LOOK ON HIS FACE...

THIS IS WHY...
...WAS SO NOT HIM.
RIGHT NOW, I'M STILL WILLING TO LET YOU BE MY GIRL-FRIEND.
...YOU CAN'T FOCUS ALL YOUR ATTENTION ON ME.
WHAT DO YOU SAY?

Argh!
That guy!
What's wrong with him?
If he doesn't like it, why can't he just yell at me as usual?
So I'm close to my brother, so what?
Why get so down about it?
That's so not like him.

It's so not Ryoki.
To look like that.
1401
TACHIBANA
If I push this, that scary mother of his will open the door...
I know that.
...say really mean things to me...
...and send me packing without letting me see him.
I totally know that, but...

DING DONG
YES?
IT'S SHINOGU.
KLAK
Odagiri
SHINOGU?
...

...HI.
COME IN.
GO AHEAD, SLUG ME IF YOU WANT. I...
...TOLD HATSUMI YOUR SECRET.
...DON'T APOLOGIZE TO *ME.*
APOLOGIZE TO *HER.*
SHE SAID IT DOESN'T MATTER IF WE'RE RELATED OR NOT.
THAT TO HER, I'M HER BROTHER NO MATTER WHAT.
SHE WAS DESPERATE... TRYING TO PROTECT MY FEELINGS.

SO...
DROP THE VENDETTA, ALL RIGHT?
HOW CAN WE MAKE IT UP TO YOU SO YOU'RE SATISFIED?
...MY OLD MAN'S COMING BACK FROM OSAKA TOMORROW.
I DON'T WANT YOU TO EVER...
...DO ANYTHING TO HURT HATSUMI AGAIN.
WTAPS

I'M SO SORRY...
...TO HAVE KEPT YOU WAITING!
HUH?!
Who is this?!
OH...
This totally beautiful...
MAID...? Since when did they...
WOULD YOU LIKE TO SEE MASTER RYOKI?
ONE MOMENT, PLEASE. I SHALL CALL HIM IMMEDIATELY.
SMILE
YIKES
Oops, couldn't help staring...
patta patta patta patta
UM!
I, UH...
KA-CHAK
HUH? A FRIEND? AND IT ISN'T SUBARU?
Okay, so now I'm here...
NO, IT ISN'T. I...SHALL BE IN THE KITCHEN.
But what do I say to him...?
WHO --

UH...
UMM...
WHAT'RE **YOU** HERE FOR?
GULP
AND WHAT THE HELL ARE YOU HOLDING?
OOPS.
Gyak! I've still got my apron on, too.
THIS IS, UH, WELL...
How embar-rassing!
I WAS JUST ABOUT TO START MAKING DINNER, AND...
SIGH

...AND WHAT?
WHAT THE HELL'S WITH YOU, ANYWAY...
...TOTALLY PISSES ME OFF!
I...
I JUST DON'T GET YOU.
YOU SAY YOU DON'T WANT TO BE MY GIRLFRIEND...
AND THEN YOU ASK ME OUT. LIKE, ON A DATE, PRACTICALLY...
AND THEN WHEN I GO, ALL YOU DO IS TALK ABOUT YOUR BROTHER.

THEN YOU TELL ME I MAKE YOUR HEART THROB...
SO I THINK YOU'RE INTO ME...
BUT THEN YOU JUST IGNORE ME AND GET ALL LOVEY-DOVEY WITH YOUR BROTHER.
LOVEY... DOVEY ...?
COME ON.
Hey...
He sounds... kinda cranky.
HE'S MY **BROTHER**, RYOKI... WE'VE ALWAYS BEEN CLOSE...
...
Until right now...
TOO CLOSE FOR COM-FORT.
WHAT WAS THAT **MOMENT** YOU GUYS HAD BACK THERE, ANYWAY?
I thought he was so scary at times like this.
He always scared me.
YOU NEVER LOOK AT **ME** LIKE THAT. EVER.
He totally terrified me.

FOR-GET THIS.
I'M NOT LETTING YOU BE MY GIRLFRIEND AFTER ALL.
TIME OUT!
But actually ...
He's really kinda...

...HUH?
WHAT DID I...
...JUST DO?
HATSUMI...

... HAS NOTHING TO DO WITH YOUR MOM.
SHE DOESN'T KNOW ANYTHING.
YOU KNOW NONE OF IT WAS HER FAULT.
...IF YOU KNOW ABOUT ME...
THEN YOU KNOW IT WAS MY FAULT...
YOU KNOW THAT, DON'T YOU?
...THAT IT ALL STARTED WHEN MY MOM...
HERE, SHINOGU-CHAN.
YOU DON'T EVER HAVE TO BE AFRAID AGAIN.
... TOOK ME IN, WITHOUT DISCUSSING IT FIRST WITH MY DAD.
THAT'S WHAT STARTED THE WHOLE MESS...
FROM TODAY ...
... THIS IS YOUR HOUSE, OKAY?
LET'S ALL LIVE TO-GETHER HERE!

IF YOU HURT HATSUMI...
...OVER SOMETHING THAT'S MY FAULT...
IF YOU LOVE HER SO MUCH, WHY DON'T YOU TELL HER?
DON'T BE... STUPID.
THAT'S NOT WHY I'M --
YOU REALLY WILL LOSE HER TO RYOKI, YOU KNOW.
YOU COOL WITH THAT?

GO FOR IT.
TAKE HER AWAY FROM HIM.
...
...

I'M...
... SORRY, I... JUST...
UH, I... WELL...
YOU WERE SO... CUTE...
PHWA
SORRY. I BETTER GO.
I...
SORRY I BOTHERED YOU...

KA-THONK
...I'M WILLING TO CUT YOU SOME SLACK...
AND IF IT'S JUST THIRTY... NO, TWENTY PERCENT OF THE TIME, I MAY EVEN LET YOU...
...THINK ABOUT YOUR BROTHER...
...AND ANY OTHER STUFF BESIDES...
...AND LET YOU BE MY GIRL-FRIEND-IN-TRAINING.

...ME.
Okay.
I'll try it.

What the maid saw...

Chapter 23

MEANWHILE...
THE TWO OF US ARE FACING OFF DOWN-STAIRS...

Omigod.

I just agreed...

...to try out being Ryoki's girlfriend-in-training (important distinction).

Actually ...
I wonder if he noticed...
...that instead of saying yes...
I just closed my eyes.

DA-DOOM
DA-DOOM

SHE ISN'T TRYING...
...TO GET AWAY...
BEFORE, SHE ALWAYS WRIGGLED AND SQUIRMED AND PUSHED ME AWAY.
ALWAYS SAID NO AND FOUGHT ME.
NOO! LET GO OF ME!
Pisses me off!
I HATE YOU!
OHHH...I GET IT. OF COURSE. I KNOW WHAT THIS IS! THIS MUST BE...
A CONSEN-SUAL KISS.
AH, CONSENT! HOW SPLENDID IT IS!

Hey!
Oh.
Uh, umm... Ooh...
Omigod! His tongue...
BLUSH
Eeeek! His tongue just...
Nn...gh! Nnnn!
Nnnnnn ...
SHWOOO

NGH!
BWONK
OW...CH! ARGH...
URR... URGH... MWOOF!
Whoa, whoa, whoaa! Hold on!
I just hit my head real hard on the floor!
Ryoki! Let go of me! I'm in total pain here!!
MWORGH MWORGH
SQUEEZ
!
MM, HA-TSUMI...
MMMM...
HATSUMI!

This is hopeless.
He's totally oblivious...
DINGDONG
GASP
DINGDONG
DINGDONG

KA-CHAK
... YES?
...OH!
YES, BUT I DON'T THINK ...
OWWWW
.... (furious)
COULD YOU... PLEASE WAIT A MOMENT?
Via intercom
WHO IS IT?!
I'M VERY SORRY, BUT...
YOUR FRIENDS... FROM THE BUILDING ...
KA-CHAK
HEY, IT'S OPEN! THEY GOT AN OPEN-DOOR POLICY HERE!
HIC!
HI THERE! GOOD EVENING! HOW YA DOING? WE'RE DOING GREAT!
KYA HA HA HA
HEEEY, HATSUMI BABY! YOU'RE HERE TOO! THAT'S JUST PERRRFECT!
YEAH, WE'RE HAVING A BLAST!

WE HEARD THAT YOUR MOM WAS OUT OF TOWN FOR A FEW DAYS? SO WE THOUGHT...
WOO HOO!
HEY, RYOKI MIGHT WANNA PARTY WITH US! HOW 'BOUT IT, RYOKI?
KOFF KOFF
SORRY 'BOUT THIS, RYO...
FIRST WE WERE JUST HAVING DINNER, BUT THEN WE HAD A FEW BEERS, AND...
HEEE HEEE
C'MON, SIS, LET'S GO...RYOKI'S GOT A BIG PRACTICE EXAM TOMORROW...
bonk!
SHUT YOUR PIE HOLE, WHO CARES?!
...
AKANE... WEREN'T YOU STUDYING FOR YOUR EXAMS...?
OMIGOD, THEY HAVE A MAID! I WANNA TRY ON THAT UNIFORM, IT'S, LIKE, SO CUUUTE!
SQUEAL SQUEAL SQUEAL
HEY, LET'S ALL GET DRESSED UP! COSTUME PARTY, YOU GUYS! LET'S GET WASTED!
GLOMP
YOU TOO, HATSUMI ...!
UH...
WELL...
ALL RIGHT.

YOU GUYS GO INTO MY ROOM AND WAIT THERE. DON'T MAKE TOO MUCH NOISE.
WE'RE GOING OUT TO GET SOME STUFF TO MUNCH ON, ALL RIGHT?
MARIKO-SAN, MY COAT. AND MY GLASSES.
WHAAT?!
WHAT A GUY! RYOKI-KUN, YOU ARE SO SWEET! ♡
OOOH
HIC
HIC
RYO...? ARE YOU SERIOUS ...?
IS THIS GONNA BE FUN OR WHAT?! HEY, LET'S GET AZUSA UP HERE TOO!
THANKS, MARIKO-SAN. WE'RE GOING.
What?
He's fine with it?!
I UNDER-STAND, SIR.
PLEASE BE CAREFUL.
smile
SLAM!
...JEEZ!

hotgimmick

WHAT A GOD DAMN PAIN IN THE ASS. (furious)
HEY! GET MOVING!
WE'RE... REALLY GOING?
THEN I BETTER GO GET MY PURSE...ARE WE GOING DOWN TO THE 7-ELEVEN?
WHO CARES ABOUT THAT?! JUST GET YOUR COAT.
HUH?
WE'RE GOING SOMEPLACE WE CAN BE ALONE.
WHAT?!

DING
LET'S SEE ...
WOO
WHERE DOES AZUSA LIVE AGAIN ...?
705...? YEAH, I THINK THAT'S RIGHT.
...I REALLY DON'T GET WHY YOU'RE HOLDING BACK LIKE THAT, I SWEAR.
HUH ...?
JUST GO AHEAD AND TELL HER, WHY DONCHA?
YOU AND HATSUMI AREN'T EVEN RELATED. SHE ISN'T REALLY YOUR SISTER.
TELL HER YOU WANT HER.

SHUP
ENOUGH, AZUSA.
I'M GOING.
I'LL SEE YOU TOMORROW...
HATSUMI'S REAL DENSE ABOUT STUFF LIKE THAT, SO SHE PROBABLY HASN'T NOTICED... BUT IF YOU ASK *ME*, IT'S TOTALLY OBVIOUS.
YOU LOOK AT HER THE SAME WAY RYOKI LOOKS AT HER, SHINOGU.
...YOU WANT HER.
YOU WANNA LOCK HER UP...
...HAVE HER ALL TO YOURSELF...
...AND DO HER. DON'T YOU?

HFF
...IF
I TOLD
HER...
WOULD
THAT
MAKE
HER
HAPPY?
IF IT
MADE
HATSUMI HAPPY,
SURE, I'D TELL
HER I LOVE HER.
I'D DO
ANYTHING.

BUT HAPPY'S THE LAST THING SHE'D BE IF I SAID SOMETHING LIKE THAT TO HER NOW.
SO... NO WAY. I'D DIE BEFORE I'D TELL HER.
I'M NOT TAKING YOUR BAIT, AZUSA.
I'M COMING BACK TOMORROW WITH MY OLD MAN, SO THINK ABOUT WHAT I SAID.
GOOD NIGHT.
TOK TOK
TOK
TOK

OH.
ASAHI...
URGH
...DID YOU HEAR --
UH...
NO, I... UMM...
HEY!
GLAD I RAN INTO YOU! I JUST GOT HERE, LIKE, RIGHT NOW, ACTUALLY!
WE'RE PARTYING! WHY DON'T YOU JOIN US, SHINOGU?! C'MON!
ME AND SUBA AND AKANE AND HATSUMI AND, LET'S SEE, RYOKI...
THUUMP!

OOPS... UH...
WE'RE...UP AT RYOKI'S PLACE AND... UH...
HA HA, WELL...
OH, BUT I GUESS YOU CAN'T COME, HUH? YOU'RE BUSY MOVING OUT, RIGHT?
GUESS YOU DON'T HAVE THE TIME...
HA HA HA

PACK-ING'S A PAIN IN THE ASS, HUH? AND THEN THE **UNPACK-ING,** MY GOD...
ASAHI.
BUT IT MUST BE GREAT TO HAVE YOUR OWN PLACE. LUCKY YOU...
...ASAHI.
HA HA...
HA...
WHY ARE YOU CRYING ...?
...IT'S OKAY...
I WON'T TELL.
I SWEAR I WON'T TELL ANYBODY, EVER.
I WON'T TELL, SHINOGU ...

WHAT'S... KEEPING THEM?
GEE, IT SURE IS TAKING MY SISTER A LONG TIME TO GET AZUSA UP HERE...
WONDER WHERE RYO AND HATSUMI WENT FOR THOSE, UM, SNACKS ...?
GLUG GLUG GLUG GLUG
WHY'D SHE HAVE TO...
...LEAVE ME ALONE WITH AKANE?
fluster
fluster
THANKS A LOT, SIS!
PHOO
HEEEY, SHUBA-ROOOO.
YOOOOW!
...HOW COME YOO'RE ALLWAY' SHO...
... WEIRD AROUN' MEEE?
巨峰果汁使用
-HI
お酒

YOO REEELY DOAN...
...LIKE MEE, HUH...?
YOO DOAN FINK I'M PRIDDY?
ORRR IZZIT MY BOOOBS?
THEY ARN'T BIG ENUF FER YOO?

FWUP
TOO SHMALL ...?
MWUSH
OOPS...! SS...SORR...
OOOH... MMMM...GO AHEAD, SQUEEZE 'EM ALL YOU WANT...
I...
I DOAN... MIND...
IF YOU WANNA DO IT, THASS FINE BY...
WHAT...

... ARE YOU SAYING?! GIRLS SHOULDN'T SAY STUFF LIKE THAT!!
BOFF
I'M...
... GETTING A DRINK OF WATER!
DABA DABA DABA DABA DABA
BUT... BUT...I THOUGHT... GUYS LIKE...
... DOING IT...
BAM DA DA DA DA BAM
HOW ...
... COME ...?

WHA... 'M I SUPPOSE TO DO NOW?
I DOAN KNOW WHAT ELSH TO DOOO...
WAIT! WAIT WAIT WAIT!
WHAT DO YOU MEAN, SOMEPLACE WE CAN BE...
... ALONE ...? C'MON...
I CAN'T!
DON'T DO THIS TO ME...
DON'T WORRY.
WE'RE GOING IN THERE FIRST...

...TO GET SOME PROTECTION. SO RELAX.
PROTECTION?!!!
JUST... HOLD ON! WAIT! HOW COME ?!
THEY'RE ALL WAITING FOR US.
SO WHY THIS, ALL OF A SUDDEN ?!
ALL OF A SUDDEN ?!
NOT TO MENTION!
WHAT THE HELL'S SO SUDDEN ABOUT IT AFTER WHAT WE WERE JUST DOING?!
YOU SAID WE COULD DO IT IF YOU BECAME MY GIRLFRIEND!
BUT I'M ONLY "IN TRAINING"!
PLUS I SO NEVER SAID THAT!
COME ON, NURSES IN TRAINING AREN'T ALLOWED TO GIVE INJECTIONS OR DO IVs OR ANY-THING!
OH YEAH? WELL, INTERNS GET TO DO ALL KINDS OF STUFF!
Like Carter in ER!
I CAN'T, RYOKI... I JUST CAN'T!
...
THE WAY WE WERE KISSING ...

...YOU'RE CRAZY IF YOU EXPECT ME TO JUST TAKE CARE OF IT BY MYSELF...
Take care of...
BUT... I JUST DON'T...
What?
OH!
OKIWA DRUGS
HATSUMI-CHAN?
IS THAT YOU, HATSUMI-CHAN?
YIPES!

OH...
MRS.... HONDA...
GOOD EVENING...
HYEEEELP
NEIGHBORS FROM THE COMPLEX!
And not just any neighbors... Mrs. T's henchwomen!
IT REALLY ISN'T SAFE FOR A YOUNG GIRL TO BE WALKING AROUND OUTSIDE AT THIS HOUR...
YOU SHOULD BE CARE-FUL...
OH... WHO'S THAT WITH YOU ...?
...
THAT'S MRS. TACHIBANA'S... RYOKI-KUN!
DOWN.
GOOD EVE-NING...
Oh no!
FWUP
WE JUST RAN INTO EACH OTHER!! SO HE'S WALKING ME HOME!
Cover up. Gotta cover up!
WE JUST BUMPED INTO EACH OTHER, RIGHT? RIGHT, RYOKI?!
OH, REALLY ...
SCRAMBLE
SCRAMBLE
WELL, TAKE CARE, THEN, BOTH OF YOU. BYE...
GOOD NIGHT!

TCH!
PHEW
HEY!
WHADDAYA MEAN, WE JUST "BUMPED INTO EACH OTHER" ...
GOOD EVENING!
PLEASE SAY HELLO TO YOUR MOTHER FOR US!
...SURE.
I'LL DO THAT.
JEEZ ...!
YOU CAN'T TAKE A STEP AROUND HERE...
... WITHOUT RUNNING INTO OUR NEIGHBORS ...
Exactly.

I agreed to be his girl-friend or whatever...
...without thinking about it too much, but...
This might be really...
I mean, seriously...
...bad news.
LET'S GO OUT TO THE STATION ...
If people see us together like this...
...they might start talking about me again, like before...
UM...
HUH?
INSIDE THE COMPLEX. AND AROUND THE NEIGH-BOR-HOOD.
IT MIGHT BE BETTER TO ACT LIKE THERE'S NOTHING BETWEEN US, YOU KNOW?
MAYBE WE SHOULD... KEEP IT A SECRET ...?
WE'RE GOING. GET UP...
I...
RYOKI ...?

GIMME A BREAK! WHERE THE HELL ELSE ARE WE SUPPOSED TO SEE EACH OTHER, YOU DOPE?!
WE GO TO DIFFERENT SCHOOLS! WE TAKE DIFFERENT TRAINS!
BUT... IF...YOUR MOTHER FINDS OUT ABOUT... US...
I... MY WHOLE FAMILY...
... COULD END UP GETTING IGNORED AGAIN... BY THE WHOLE COMPLEX...
...YOU SURE...
...THAT ISN'T JUST AN EXCUSE?
TO GET AWAY FROM ME?

NO... OF COURSE IT ISN'T --
YARGH !
...YOU SAID A GIRL-FRIEND ...
...IS SOMETHING YOU BECOME WHEN YOU FALL IN LOVE WITH SOMEONE. RIGHT?

SO TELL ME YOU LOVE ME.
YOU DO THAT, I'LL KEEP OUR RELATIONSHIP A SECRET.
SAY YOU LOVE ME.
COME ON.

SAY IT.
...Oh no.
DA-DOOM
This is bad news... I know that.
I shouldn't say it... I know that.
Oh god, I can't even look at him.

Was Ryoki always so...
... dazzling ...? He's blinding me...
...HATSUMI?
WHAT ARE YOU DOING HERE?
THUUMP!

OH!
FWUP
MOM!!
OH...
GOOD EVENING...
OH MY... IS THAT RYOKI-KUN?!
OH MY!
GOODNESS GRACIOUS!
WHAT'S GOING ON?!
WHAT'RE THE TWO OF YOU DOING OUT HERE SO LATE...?
UM...
WELL... UH...
WE WERE ALL STUDYING TOGETHER.
Huh?!
MY MOTHER'S GONE THIS WEEK, SO WE'RE UP AT MY PLACE.
SUBARU AND YOUR YOUNGER DAUGHTER, TOO.
THE TWO OF US JUST CAME OUT TO BUY A FEW SNACKS.
He's so smart.
I SEE...
PHEW
WELL...I WAS AT A FAREWELL PARTY FOR WORK, MYSELF. AND NOW LOOK AT THE TIME!

GWIP!
SO... COME ON, HATSUMI. IT'S TIME TO GO HOME!
YOU'VE STUDIED LONG ENOUGH!
I'M SURE YOU'D LIKE TO HAVE YOUR HOUSE BACK TO YOURSELF, RYOKI-KUN. HOO HOO HOO!
...NOT AT ALL.
BUT WE'LL BREAK IT UP.
I'LL SEND THE OTHERS HOME AS WELL. IT IS LATE.
THEN I'LL GO WITH YOU TO GET AKA --
SHE'LL BE FINE!
SHE JUST HAS TO RIDE THE ELEVATOR DOWN!
WELL. I'LL BE GOING HOME FROM THAT SIDE.
Oh no.
Is this okay with him? We were in the middle of something.
He isn't mad ??
GRR
DAMN IT!
IF I'D KNOWN THIS WAS GOING TO HAPPEN, I WOULD'VE DRAGGED HER BEHIND SOME BUSHES IN THE PARK!!!
HEY.
HA-TSUMI. WE'RE GOING.

I knew it. He IS mad.
He hasn't looked back even once.
HATSUMI!
OH.
SORRY. I'M COMING.
...HMPH.
DOESN'T EVEN LOOK BACK...
PISSES ME OFF!
HEY, HATSUMI...

UMM...
I DON'T MEAN TO PRY, BUT...
YOU WOULDN'T BE...
GOING OUT WITH RYOKI OR ANYTHING LIKE THAT...
... WOULD YOU...?
KATHONK!
...NO ...
...I'M NOT...
OF COURSE NOT...
THANK GOD!
PHEW
I KNOW YOU'VE BEEN AFRAID OF HIM SINCE CHILDHOOD, SO IT DIDN'T...
... SEEM VERY LIKELY ...
BUT THE VERY THOUGHT OF IT...JUST WHEN EVERYTHING HAD FINALLY SETTLED DOWN WITH SHINOGU BECOMING RYOKI'S TUTOR...
JUST IMAGINE WHAT HIS MOTHER WOULD DO TO US...

I DON'T EVER WANT TO GO THROUGH THAT KIND OF UNPLEASANTNESS AGAIN...
SO PLEASE, HATSUMI...
DON'T EVEN THINK ABOUT DATING RYOKI, OKAY?
HA HA HA HA HA
BAM

OH! MASTER RYOKI...
YOU'RE HOME SO EARLY.
I...PARDON ME, BUT I HAD ASSUMED YOU WOULD BE RETURNING MUCH LATER.

SIGH

...?
YOU ALWAYS SIGH LIKE THAT WHEN YOU COME OUT OF THE BATHROOM?
WORGH!
OH MY GOD! **RYO!**
SORRY! I DIDN'T MEAN TO DO THAT IN YOUR BATHROOM BUT...
HUH?
OH, NOTHING, NOTHING! JUST FORGET I SAID ANYTHING... SORRY!!

WHATEVER. LOOK, PARTY'S OVER. TAKE JUNIOR HERE AND GO HOME, ALL RIGHT?

Cried herself to sleep, apparently.

WHAT?!

ME?! BUT I FINALLY MANAGED TO GET IT DOWN...UH, OOPS...

HUH?!

Oh god.

Now what do I do?

HERE YOU ARE.

302

NARITA

SHINOGU ...
Take Hikaru, will you?
OH, GOOD. YOU'RE HOME. DID YOU GET A CALL FROM YOUR FATHER?
UH, YEAH...
...WHAT IS IT?
YOU DON'T LOOK SO GREAT.
HUH? I'M FINE...
The way I'm feeling...
IT'S... NOTHING. REALLY...
I don't know if I can have that talk with Dad tomorrow ...

Hot Gimmick

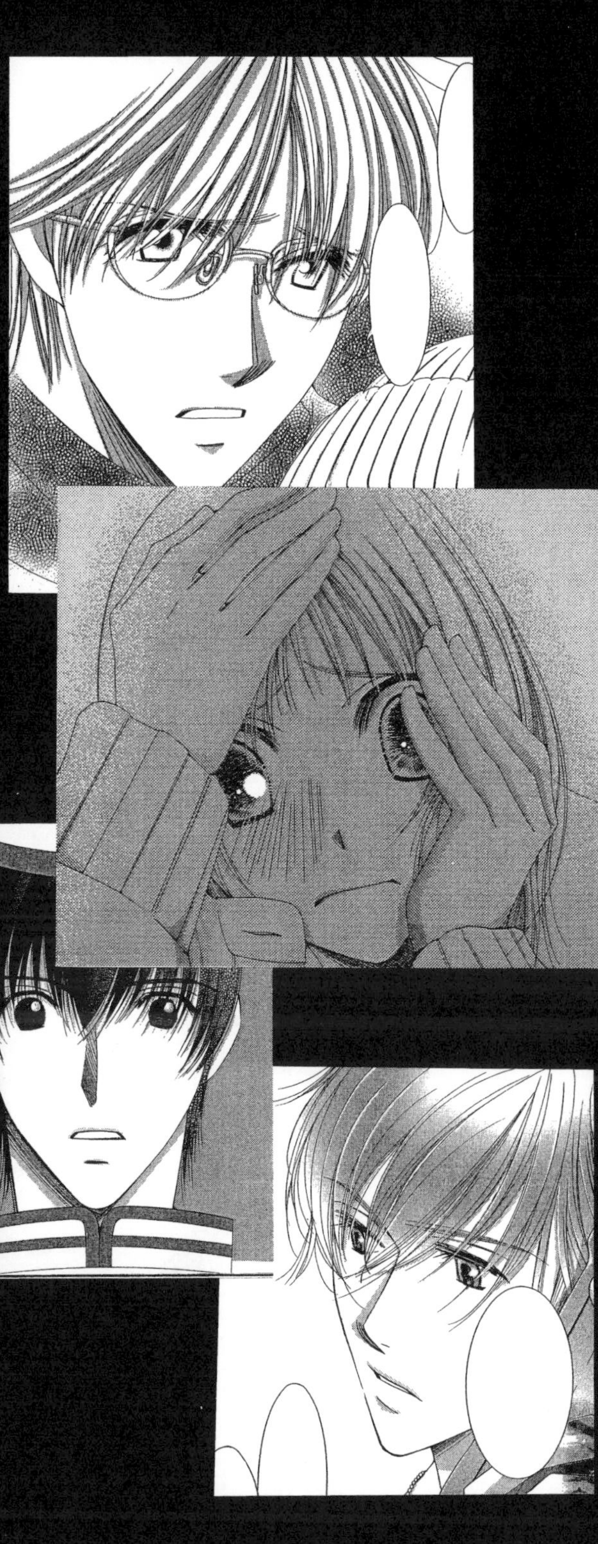

vol.6

MIKI AIHARA

Chapter 24
AZUSA
Monotone designer suit, simply accentuated with a scarf.
Leather jacket: ¥150,000
Shirt: ¥15,000 Pants: ¥22,000
Shoes ¥25,000 / all from agnes b. homme
Scarf: ¥48,000 / Burberry

hotgimmick

SEE THAT KID OVER THERE? THAT'S AZUSA ODAGIRI.

THE ONE WHO MOVED HERE FROM TOKYO.

HIS DAD DIVORCED HIS MOM BECAUSE SHE HAD AN AFFAIR.

WHAT'S AN "AFFAIR"?

IT MEANS SHE HAD A LOVER, STUPID. THAT'S WHAT MY MOM SAID.

MY MOMMY SAID I CAN'T PLAY WITH HIM, CUZ HIS MOTHER'S A BAD LADY.

ME TOO.

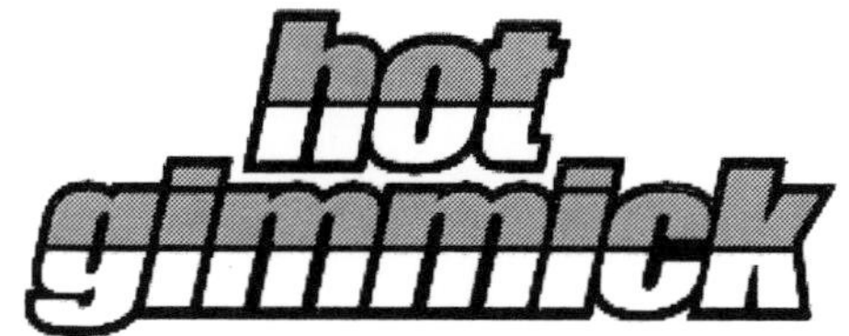

THAT'S THE NEW KID IN HOME-ROOM FOUR.
OH, REALLY? HE'S PRETTY CUTE.
FORGET IT. HIS MOM'S THIS TOTAL --
WHAT? NO WAY... REALLY?
REALLY... THAT MIHO-SAN!
JUST SUDDENLY SHOWING UP HERE LIKE THIS, WITH THAT CHILD OF HERS, TOO.
MY HUSBAND'S SO SWEET ON HIS SISTER. OF COURSE NOBODY ASKED ME HOW I FEEL ABOUT IT. I MEAN, JUST BECAUSE SHE GREW UP IN THIS HOUSE DOESN'T MEAN SHE CAN MOVE RIGHT BACK IN...
AND YOU KNOW I'M THE ONE WHO'S GOING TO END UP LOOKING AFTER THAT BOY.
YES INDEED, MA'AM.
HFF
FRANKLY, THEY'RE A REAL BURDEN. LOOK AT THOSE DOCTOR'S BILLS SHE'S RUNNING UP. WHO DO YOU THINK IS GOING TO PAY THEM?
SHWA

AZUSA. YOU'RE BACK.
HOW DID YOU LIKE YOUR NEW SCHOOL? THINK YOU'LL FIT IN?
YEAH. IT WAS REALLY FUN!
DO YOU THINK YOU'LL MAKE FRIENDS ...?
SURE. EVERYBODY'S REALLY NICE TO ME. I'LL BE FINE!
WHAT ABOUT YOU, MOMMY? HOW'RE YOU FEELING TODAY?
I'M FEELING VERY WELL TODAY. NO TEMPERATURE OR ANYTHING.
I'LL BE FINE.

AS LONG AS MY MOM'S SMILING, I'LL BE FINE.

HEY, IS IT TRUE THAT YOUR MOM...
...GOT DIVORCED FOR HAVING AN AFFAIR?
GRANDPA SAYS HE WON'T EVEN SEE HER, CUZ SHE'S SUCH A LOOSE WOMAN.
HE SAID EVEN THOUGH YOU'RE HIS GRANDCHILD TOO, HE LOVES US BETTER.
HA HA, SO THERE!
HA HA HA HA
HE SAID YOU TWO ARE THE SHAME OF THE SHIRABASHI FAMILY!

I DON'T WANT THAT WHORE'S CHILD SITTING AT OUR TABLE.
THAT MIHO, GETTING HERSELF DIVORCED LIKE THAT...
WHAT A BLOODY DISGRACE. HOW THE HELL DO I EXPLAIN THIS TO OUR RELA-TIVES?
TELL HER SHE'S NOT TO LEAVE THE ANNEX, GOT THAT?!

I'LL BE FINE.

HEY, AZUSA. DID YOU KNOW...

...THAT IT'S OKAY TO DO THE NASTY IF YOU'RE COUSINS?

...STOP IT, AKI-CHAN. SOMEONE'LL SEE US.
IF YOU DON'T DO WHAT I SAY...
...I'LL TELL MY MOTHER TO SEND YOUR MOM TO A HOSPITAL.
ONE THAT'S REALLY FAR AWAY! YOU DON'T MIND?
... DON'T ...
SO KISS ME THEN. C'MON.
AFTER ALL, YOU ARE THE BEST-LOOKING GUY IN THE WHOLE TOWN ...
I'M GONNA TELL ALL MY FRIENDS!
BAM
H-HEY!
WHAT THE HELL ARE YOU KIDS DOING?!
D-DADDY! YOU DON'T UNDERSTAND!
IT WAS AZUSA... HE FORCED ME TO...
DIRTY LITTLE BASTARD!
THWACK
LIKE MOTHER, LIKE SON! YOU'RE BOTH SHAMELESS!
MOM ...
I'LL...
...BE FINE.

YOUR FEVER ISN'T GOING DOWN...
YOU HAVE TO EAT SOMETHING, MOM. HAVE SOME PORRIDGE, AT LEAST.
YOU LISTEN-ING, MOM?
MOM.
...I'M FINE... SOON...
VERY SOON...HE'S GOING TO COME GET ME...
HUH?
BUT MOM... YOU KNOW DAD ISN'T...
HE PROM-ISED.
HE PROMISED ME HE'D COME...
MOM...
WHO ARE YOU WAITING FOR, MOM?

WHO...
BRRRING
... ARE YOU WAITING FOR ...?
BRRRING
BRRRING
CHAK
HELLO?! AZUSA?!

OH, HI...
HEY! YOU'RE SUPPOSED TO BE BRIGHT-EYED AND BUSHY-TAILED! YOU **ARE** UP, AREN'T YOU?!
YOU'RE ON LOCATION TONIGHT, REMEMBER?! COME ON, LET'S WAKE UP!
I'LL DRIVE OVER THERE TO GET YOU AROUND FOUR, SO JUST MAKE SURE YOU'RE PACKED AND READY TO...
OH, SORRY, RINA.
I'LL GET TO THE AIRPORT BY MYSELF. I WON'T BE LATE, PROMISE.
I, UH...
...TOLD SOMEONE I'D MEET THEM TODAY.
DRRR DRRR DRRR DRRR DRRR DRRR
THOK!

Urgh.
Didn't sleep very well last night.
...Too much stuff happened yesterday...
Shinogu moved out of the house...
...for real.
And I heard the truth about Dad.
And...
And...
BLUSH

KA-CHAK
I don't know.
Was that really a good idea...? Becoming his "girlfriend-in-training"...
OH, GOOD MORNING. AWFUL EARLY, FOR YOU ANYWAY.
MWOR-NIN...
WHAT'S GOING ON TODAY? FIRST SHINOGU, NOW YOU.
HE WENT OUT TO MEET YOUR FATHER AT THE STATION.
YAWN
HE'S TRYING TO BUTTER HIM UP SO HE'LL SAY OKAY ABOUT HIS MOVING OUT.
IT'S SO RARE FOR SHINOGU TO GO TO SUCH LENGTHS TO GET WHAT HE WANTS.
HM? HA-TSUMI...?
SLAM!
Shinogu's going to tell Dad about Azusa.
That's why he went out to meet him (so Mom won't be there).
No fair, sneaking off without me like that.
OH...

MISS NARITA FROM #302.
HUH ?
UH... OH!!
YOU'RE THE TACHI-BANAS'...
Maid!!
SMILE
PLEASE PARDON ME FOR STOPPING YOU.
I CAME TO BRING YOU THIS. YOU LEFT IT BEHIND YESTERDAY EVENING.
OH...
THANK YOU! AND I'M SORRY THAT YOU HAD TO COME DOWN JUST FOR...
OH NO, IT WAS NO TROUBLE AT ALL.
UMM... IS THIS...
... FROM RYOKI ?

SSSSSS
NO. MASTER RYOKI IS STILL ASLEEP.
IT APPEARS HE GOT QUITE EXHAUSTED YESTERDAY.
GIGGLE GIGGLE
HE SLEPT VERY DEEPLY ALL NIGHT.
WELL, IF YOU'LL EXCUSE ME...
DEEEP
OH, OF COURSE ...
THANK YOU AGAIN, MARIKO-SAN.

... Mariko-san...? Wait a second ...
How come I know her name?
Oh ...
MARIKO-SAN, MY COAT. AND MY GLASSES.
THANKS, MARIKO-SAN. WE'RE GOING.
He slept very deeply all night.
....
Okay. Let's not think about that right now.
Right now...
I need to find Shinogu.
DING

HIYA. TALK ABOUT GREAT TIMING!
UH... HI...
SORRY ABOUT YESTERDAY. Y'KNOW, THE STUFF I SAID ABOUT YOUR BROTHER.
HEY, I'LL SHOW YOU SOME-THIN'. BY WAY OF APOLOGY.
COME WITH ME.
I JUST HEARD FROM SHINOGU.
OH...

HE SAID HE'S WITH YOUR DAD, AND TO COME MEET THEM.
GOTTA HAND IT TO HIM.
THEY'RE AT CAFE BRAN, YOU KNOW IT? ON A BACK STREET ON THE OTHER SIDE OF THE STATION? GOOD CHANCE NOBODY FROM THE COMPLEX WILL SEE US THERE.
café bran
café bran
hotgimmick

I'LL BE WORKING, SO I CAN PAY THE RENT AND LIVING EXPENSES MYSELF.
PLUS I'VE SAVED UP ENOUGH TO LAST ME ABOUT A YEAR ANYWAY.
BUT... I'LL NEED YOU TO PAY MY TUITION FOR A LITTLE LONGER...
I'M SORRY TO BE ASKING YOUR PER-MISSION AFTER I'VE ALREADY MOVED OUT...
BUT I REALLY HOPE YOU'LL UNDER-STAND, DAD...
SIGH
...I WISH YOU'D HAVE WAITED, AT LEAST UNTIL I WAS TRANS-FERRED BACK TO TOKYO.
I NEED YOU TO LOOK AFTER YOUR MOTHER AND THE OTHER CHILDREN ...
I'LL LOOK AFTER THEM!
DON'T BE SILLY. YOUR NEW PLACE IS AN HOUR AWAY.
I WILL.

I SWEAR I'LL LOOK AFTER THEM.

...SHINOGU...

THE REASON YOU MOVED OUT.

IS IT REALLY ...

... BECAUSE YOU WANT TO LIVE ON YOUR OWN?

OR IS IT BE-CAUSE ...

DAD.

I HAVE SOME-THING ELSE TO ASK YOU.

...I WANT YOU TO TALK TO AZUSA ODAGIRI.

SEE, I HEARD... THAT THE WOMAN YOU WERE SEEING THAT TIME, WAS AZUSA'S MOTHER.

...DID YOU HEAR THAT FROM AZUSA?
SO THEN... DO YOUR MOTHER AND THE REST OF THE FAMILY ...?
NO, ONLY ME AND HATSUMI KNOW ABOUT IT.
AZUSA REALLY HAS IT IN FOR YOU OVER THAT, AND...
... SINCE YOU'RE NOT AROUND, HE'S BEEN TAKING IT OUT ON HATSUMI. HARASSING HER AND STUFF.
HATSUMI ?!
YEAH. SHE'S BEEN HIDING IT, BUT I...
WELL... I JUST WANT IT TO STOP...

...SO...
DAD. PLEASE. SIT DOWN AND TALK TO AZUSA.
I HAVEN'T HEARD THE DETAILS...
BUT...
I DON'T THINK AZUSA'S THE TYPE THAT WOULD SAY SOMETHING LIKE THAT WITHOUT ANY GROUNDS...
DAD...
RELAX.
I CAME BACK TO TOKYO TODAY FOR TWO REASONS.
ONE WAS TO TALK TO YOU.
THE OTHER WAS TO APOLOGIZE TO AZUSA.

KLATTER
AZU... HATSUMI!
SHUK

HATSUMI.
COME OVER HERE.
NOW.
GWIP
HEY... SHINO-GU...
I TOLD YOU TO KEEP HATSUMI OUT OF THIS!
...AZUSA ...

...WHO...
...TOLD YOU ABOUT THIS...?
...MY MOM'S DIARY...
...NEVER ACTUALLY MENTIONED THE GUY BY NAME.
SO I SPENT ALL THE MONEY I EARNED MODELING ON DETECTIVE AGENCIES.
WHEN I SAW YOUR FATHER...
...IN OSAKA THE OTHER DAY, HE DIDN'T SEEM TO...
MY DAD DOESN'T KNOW ANYTHING.
AND ANYWAY, HE DUMPED MY MOM SO...
WHO CARES, ANYWAY. JUST HURRY UP AND APOLO-GIZE.
YOU SAID THAT'S WHAT YOU'RE HERE FOR. TO APOLOGIZE TO ME.
APOLO-GIZING MEANS... YOU ADMIT IT.
YOU ADMIT IT'S YOUR FAULT THAT MY MOTHER DIED.

...YES, THAT'S RIGHT.
I'M VERY SORRY ABOUT THAT.
DAD.

So...
It's true. Dad and Azusa's mom really were...
...YOU THINK...
...THAT'S ENOUGH? THAT ABSOLVES YOU FROM EVERY-THING?

MY MOM WAITED AND WAITED.
SHE'D STARE OUT THE WINDOW ALL DAY, WAITING FOR YOU.
EVEN AFTER SHE GOT TOO WEAK TO EAT OR TAKE HER MEDICINE ...
SHE JUST ...
... KEPT WAITING.
AND NOW ALL YOU CAN SAY IS ***YOU'RE SORRY***?
NO EXCUSES, NO EXPLANA-TIONS, NO NOTHING?
COME ON... THAT ISN'T FAIR.
I...
WHAT I...

I'M TERRIBLY SORRY.
THERE'S NOTHING ELSE I CAN SAY...

...
DAD ...?

...!

GIMME A BREAK...

THAT AIN'T CLOSE TO ENOUGH!

tup

HATSU...

...DAD...

THAT WASN'T ...
... REALLY THE TRUTH, WAS IT...?
HUFF
HUFF

...WHY...
...ARE YOU FOLLOWING ME...?
CUZ...
HUFF HUFF
CUZ... YOU...
BECAUSE ...
KUMATAN
Dear Azusa,
How are you? I am fine
Today we had a bazaar
the complex. Ryok
hit me with
Ichihara City
To Mister Azusa Oda
From Hatsumi Narita

YOU LOOKED...
...LIKE YOU WERE ABOUT TO CRY...

...I THOUGHT I'D HATE YOU.
THE HAPPY NARITA FAMILY. SEEING YOU GUYS ENJOYING LIFE...
... AFTER ALL MY MOM WENT THROUGH BECAUSE OF YOUR DAD.
LIKE, SCREW YOU GUYS, YOU KNOW?
SO I WANTED TO PAY YOU BACK.
MESS UP YOUR LIVES AND SCREW YOU UP.
I WANTED TO HURT YOU REALLY BAD, HATSUMI. YOU KNOW THAT, OF COURSE.

BUT IT DIDN'T WORK OUT LIKE THAT.
I JUST CAN'T HATE YOU.
WHEN I SEE YOU OR SHINOGU LOOKING HURT OR SAD...
I DON'T KNOW... IT JUST GETS ME DOWN.
...I THOUGHT IF I GOT HIM DOWN ON HIS KNEES LIKE THAT...
I'D FEEL A LOT BETTER.
AZUSA...

FUNNY...
I DON'T FEEL BETTER AT ALL...

Everything's supposed to be cleared up now, but...

I don't feel better at all.

hotgimmick

LEFT BEHIND AT THE CAFE...

Chapter 25

GOOD MORNING!

COLD TODAY, ISN'T IT?

SURE IS. LOOKS LIKE SNOW, DOESN'T IT?

WELL, IT IS DECEMBER ALREADY. MY, THE YEAR JUST ZIPPED BY.

YOU CAN SAY THAT AGAIN.

GOOD MORNING.

SO YOU'LL BE BACK AGAIN THE WEEK AFTER NEXT. WON'T YOU BE LONELY SPENDING CHRISTMAS ALONE?
DON'T BE SILLY.
BE CAREFUL YOU DON'T CATCH COLD.
BYE-BYE, DADDEEE!
BYE, DAAAD!
Cut her bangs.
...
After that...
I never was able to talk to Dad after all.
I just couldn't do it.
Plus he seemed to be avoiding me, too.
Azusa.
I keep seeing the way he looked that day...
DINGDONG

KA-CHAK
GOOD MORNING, TORU-SAN.
OH, MR. ODAGIRI!
Shwa
MMGH? (What?)
MMGH MGH MMGH MGH? (What's the matter?)
I THOUGHT WE MIGHT LEAVE TOGETHER, SO I CAME BY.
OH, HOW NICE OF YOU!
AND ANYWAY, I WANTED TO SAY THANK YOU FOR BEING SO GOOD TO MY SON, MRS. NARITA.
DROP THE "SAN," ODAGIRI. IT ISN'T NECES-SARY.
I'M SORRY, BUT THAT'S WHAT I ALWAYS CALLED YOU IN COLLEGE. HARD TO CHANGE YEARS OF HABIT!
SPEAKING OF AZUSA, I HEARD HE'S OFF ON LOCATION AGAIN FOR A FEW DAYS.
YES, HE IS...I DON'T KNOW HOW THAT SON OF MINE IS GOING TO FINISH HIGH SCHOOL. HA HA!
Dad.
You big coward.
WELL, AT LEAST HE'S WORKING HARD AT SOMETHING! AND HE'S DOING SO WELL!
HA HA HA HA

How ...
How can he just stand there talking to Azusa's father like nothing happened?
And in front of Mom, too.
But then...
How am I any different?
I can't tell Mom about it...
Don't stress out about it.

Now it's between Dad and Azusa.
So don't fret over it.
None of this is your fault, after all.
HATSUMI...
YOU'RE TOO NICE...
No I'm not, Shinogu.
I'm just a big coward, like Dad.
I'm only keeping it a secret from Mom and Akane...
...because I don't want my family to fall apart.
HA-TSUMI! WAIT UP!
LET'S WALK TO THE STATION TOGETHER. WHAT'S THE BIG HURRY, ANYWAY?
AKANE...
LISTEN TO THIS!
DAD TOTALLY PISSES ME OFF.
HE SAID IF I HAVE LOUSY SCORES ON MY FINALS, HE'S GONNA SEND ME TO CRAM SCHOOL. DOESN'T THAT SUCK?
He's never even home, ya know?

YEAH... THAT'S A TOTAL DRAG, COMING FROM DAD, ESPECIALLY.
I KNOW, HUH? HEY, DON'T YOU HAVE FINALS SOON YOURSELF, HATSUMI? BETTER WATCH OUT!
HEY, I KNOW...
GET RYOKI TO HELP YOU STUDY!
OH...
MORNING...
HI, RYOKI-KUN! HATSUMI NEEDS HELP STUDYING FOR HER FINALS.
SHINOGU'S GONE, SO SHE'S UP A CREEK! WHY DON'T YOU HELP HER?
...OH...

DA-DOOM
...FINALS?
NO PROBLEM, I'M FINE.
I CAN STUDY PERFECTLY WELL BY MYSELF!!
Omi-god.
Ever since that time...
I can't look at Ryoki's face up close. I mean...
...
HEY, HER HAIR'S DIFFER-ENT.

I don't know...
I feel all embarrassed, kinda, around him.
...
...UH...
THANKS, YESTERDAY. ABOUT THE LADLE...
distance
THE LADLE?
YOU KNOW...THE ONE I LEFT... AT YOUR HOUSE...
YOUR UH, MAID... BROUGHT IT DOWN...
OH.
YOU MEAN MARIKO-SAN.
Oh yeah. Of course. That's why I knew her name.
It's because Ryoki always calls her that.
YOU'RE PRETTY CLOSE TO HER, AREN'T YOU...CALLING HER BY HER FIRST NAME LIKE THAT ...
MUMBLE MUMBLE
I didn't catch that
HM? DIDJA SAY SOME-THING?
UH, NO...
I DIDN'T SAY ANYTHING!!

Why should that bother me, anyway?
Especially when I've got a million other things on my mind...
...WELL, THEN LET ME ASK YOU SOMETHING.
HFFooo
ARE YOU JERKING ME AROUND?
WHAT THE HELL'S WITH THIS DISTANCE?!
NOT TO MENTION, YOU HAVEN'T LOOKED ME IN THE EYE ONCE THIS MORNING!!
WHAT KIND OF GIRLFR--
BUT WE AGREED TO ACT LIKE THERE'S NOTHING BETWEEN US INSIDE THE COMPLEX!
NO WE DIDN'T.
BECAUSE YOU NEVER SAID IT.

SNAP
HUH ...?
SAID WHAT?
BONK!
FIGURE IT OUT YOURSELF!
3 pocket dictionaries inside
YOU DON'T COME, I'M GONNA TELL YOUR MOTHER ABOUT US.
HEYYYY... THAT HURT...
AND THEN COME MEET ME AT THE HIGASHIOKA LIBRARY IN NIKOTAMA. FOUR-THIRTY TODAY.
OWWWW
YOU BETTER BE THERE. ON TIME.
WHAT ...?

WHAT...? BUT BUT BUT... WAIT!
YOU GOTTA STUDY FOR THOSE FINALS, RIGHT?
OH, AND...
YOU SURE YOU WANNA BE TALKING TO ME HERE SO LOUD?
OOPS ...!
GLANCE
GLANCE
I have to admit...
What with all that's happened with Azusa, and Dad, and Shinogu...
... Not to mention Ryoki...
I haven't been studying at all.
HEY HATSUMI, YOU BEEN STUDYING?
HELL NO
ALL RIGHT, GOOD GIRL! JOIN THE CLUB!

JUST SO LONG AS I DON'T FAIL... REMEDIAL CLASSES TOTALLY SUCK.
WHO CARES, ANYWAY? IT'S NOT LIKE ANYBODY FROM OUR SCHOOL GOES TO COLLEGE ANY-WAY. AT LEAST NONE OF THE HARD ONES.
Until now...
...Shinogu always helped me out...
UMBRO
So I managed to barely get by with a C average.
No no no!! I can do it myself. I have to.
Shinogu just moved into his new place. He's too busy.
Plus he's got other things to worry about.
I can study by myself...

Don't think about that.
Stop thinking about Azusa.
Right now I really need to study.
glance glance
I've never been here before.
I guess not that many people know about this place...
There's an empty seat.
Who says I have to wait for Ryoki? I'm going to sit down and...
YANK

NOT OVER THERE. THIS WAY.
HEY...
RYOKI ?!
stride
stride
HEY... LET GO OF ME.
WHAT IF SOME-BODY SEES US ...?
TELL THEM WE'RE STUDYING TOGETHER. WHAT'S THE BIG DEAL? THIS IS A LIBRARY.
PLUS, THIS IS TWO STATIONS AWAY FROM HOME. NOBODY WE KNOW COMES HERE ANYWAY.
GLEEM
THERE. TOTAL PRIVACY.

...
MUCH CLOSER TOGETHER
...UMM...
IT'S... A LITTLE TIGHT... WOULDN'T YOU SAY ...?
WHADDAYA EXPECT, WE'RE SITTING IN A PLACE MADE FOR ONE PERSON.
So move to a bigger table.
Why do we have to sit here in the first place?
OH WELL, JUST IGNORE HIM.
GOTTA STUDY! LET'S GO!
OKAY... FROM PAGE 36...
TO... PAGE 45...

nyuk nyuk
tweek
WH...
WHAT?
FWIP
DON'T YOU...HAVE TO STUDY FOR YOUR FINALS, RYOKI...?
HUH?
ARE YOU KIDDING ME? WHY WOULD I WASTE MY TIME ON THAT CRAP?
Huh?

CRAP...? WASTE YOUR TIME...?
I THOUGHT YOU HAD FINALS COMING UP...
YEAH, SO? ALL YOU HAVE TO DO TO ACE 'EM IS LISTEN IN CLASS.
WHO NEEDS TO STUDY FOR THAT STUFF?
IT'S SO EASY.
I THINK I HATE HIM AFTER ALL...
SOB SOB
This is why I don't like smart people...
YOU GO AHEAD AND STUDY...
NOT THAT IT'S GONNA MAKE MUCH DIFFERENCE, WITH THAT DIM BRAIN OF YOURS.
Oh yeah?
We'll see about that.
Stop staring at me right up close like that!
How'm I supposed to concentrate?

On top of which ...
HEY...
STOP IT...
...WHAT?
I CAN'T TOUCH MY OWN GIRL-FRIEND?
IN TRAINING. YOU SAID "IN TRAINING" ...
THAT'S WHY I'M HOLDING BACK AND ONLY TOUCHING YOU.

HOLDING... BACK...?

HEY...!

YOU SAID...

...YOU WERE GONNA...
...HOLD BACK...
CAN'T. I TAKE IT BACK.
I WANNA DO IT WITH YOU.
My mind...
I WANNA DO IT.
WITH YOU.
...is going blank.
HATSUMI.

THWUMP
I HAVE TO...HAVE TO... STUDY!
I MEAN, I'M GONNA BE IN SERIOUS TROUBLE IF I DON'T, REALLY.
Oh no. Come on.
MY MOM'S GONNA BE SO MAD AT ME IF I FLUNK.
PLUS, I...
... REALLY DON'T WANT TO TAKE REMEDIAL CLASSES ...
Oh no. What's going on?
I MEAN, IF THAT HAPPENED, THERE GOES MY WINTER VACATION.
WHICH WOULD, LIKE, REALLY SUCK.
Why am I blushing like this...?
Argh! What am I blabbering on about?!!
SO I REALLY NEED TO STUD--
OKAY.
HUH?
I'LL RAISE YOUR ODDS.

HUH ...?
WHAT SUBJECTS? SHOW ME WHAT PAGES THE EXAMS COVER.
UMM... ERR... HUH?
I SAID, SHOW ME.
HERE!
Ryo...ki?
OKAY, MATH... THIS RIGHT HERE. STUDY THIS FORMULA. AND THIS ONE.
JUST LEARN THOSE, PRACTICE A FEW OF THESE PROBLEMS HERE, AND YOU'VE ALREADY GOT A 60% SCORE FOR SURE.
WHAT ABOUT ENGLISH? ...LET'S SEE...
RIGHT. MEMORIZE THIS PASSAGE HERE. THE WHOLE THING. IT'LL COME UP.
CLASSICAL JAPANESE... HMM. OKAY, THIS HERE. AND...
WHEEZE WHEEZE
PHLAP!
WELL.
THAT'S ABOUT IT. STUDY WHAT I TOLD YOU, AND YOUR CLASS RANKING WILL GO UP TWENTY PLACES. GUARANTEED.
Ha ha ha! Surely you jest...
AS... IF!
...IN RETURN FOR WHICH...

YOU GIVE ME ONE DAY OF YOUR VACA-TION.
THAT'S ONE DAY... AND ONE NIGHT.
OKAY, SO IT'S A DEAL!
FFF... FWA HA HA HA
HA HA HA HA

The stuff this guy comes up with...
Argh!
I'M... HOME...
AKANE! I JUST DON'T BELIEVE THIS!
WHAAAT?
DON'T "WHAT" ME! AND DRINKING ON SATURDAY NIGHT WHEN YOU WERE SUPPOSED TO BE STUDYING!
THREE Fs?! I DON'T EVEN KNOW WHAT TO SAY... THIS IS SIMPLY MORTIFYING!
BUT MOMMMM... THE MATH TEST COVERED, LIKE, A ZILLION PAGES...
NO EXCUSES, AKANE!
AND WITH YOUR SENIOR HIGH ENTRANCE EXAMS COMING UP NEXT YEAR!
I'M... CHANGING...
HATSUMI!

GLARE
YOU BETTER PASS ALL YOUR FINALS, YOU HEAR ME?!
IF YOU GET A SINGLE F...
WE JUST CANNOT AFFORD TO SEND TWO OF YOU TO CRAM SCHOOL, ALL RIGHT? SO YOU BETTER DO WELL.
UH...
YEAH...

...If my grades go down, Mom's gonna kill me.
But if my grades go up...
BLUSH
...AND ONE NIGHT.
What do I do...?

Oh my god.
There is no way I can do that.
* Wednesday. The day Shinogu tutors Ryoki.

...UH, RYOKI?
DON'T YOU HAVE FINALS RIGHT NOW...?
YEAH, WE HAD ENGLISH AND PHYSICS TODAY.
I JUST CHECKED MY ANSWERS A MINUTE AGO. GOT 100% ON BOTH.
OH... GREAT...
AC-TUALLY ...
ABOUT THE OTHER DAY...
THE THING ABOUT AZUSA AND MY OLD MAN.
I GUESS HATSUMI GOT YOU INVOLVED IN THAT TOO, BUT...
WELL, WE ALL MET AND TALKED, SO IT'S MORE OR LESS SETTLED NOW...
WHAT-EVER.
JUST DON'T TELL MY MOM ABOUT IT, RIGHT?
WHAT... EVER?
WHAT'S IT GOT TO DO WITH ME?
HATSUMI'S THE ONLY ONE I'M INTERESTED IN, ANYWAY.

...

LUCKY YOU.

HUH?

OH, NOTHING.

SPEAKING OF HATSUMI... SHE SHOULD BE HOME SOON. I THINK SHE GOT HER FINALS BACK TODAY.

HOPE SHE ISN'T TOO BUMMED OUT...

SMIRK

DOUBT IT.

2-A
NEXT.
NARITA. COME ON UP.
tremble
tremble
tremble
YOU STUDIED REAL HARD THIS TIME! GOOD JOB.
SEE? JUST PUT IN A LITTLE EFFORT AND LOOK WHAT YOU CAN DO!
I TALKED TO YOUR OTHER TEACHERS, AND IT SOUNDS LIKE YOUR GRADES IMPROVED ALL AROUND.
WOULDN'T BE SURPRISED IF YOUR CLASS RANKING WENT UP TWENTY, THIRTY PLACES...

HI...
I'M, UM, HOME...
Mom's gonna be thrilled.
I'll probably shoot up in the family ranking too... but...

OMIGOD! WAS TODAY...
... WEDNESDAY ...?
HI, HATSUMI.

DID YOU GET YOUR FINALS BACK? HOW'D YOU DO...? MOM WAS KINDA WORRIED...
SORRY I COULDN'T HELP YOU STUDY THIS TIME...
UH...
YEAH...

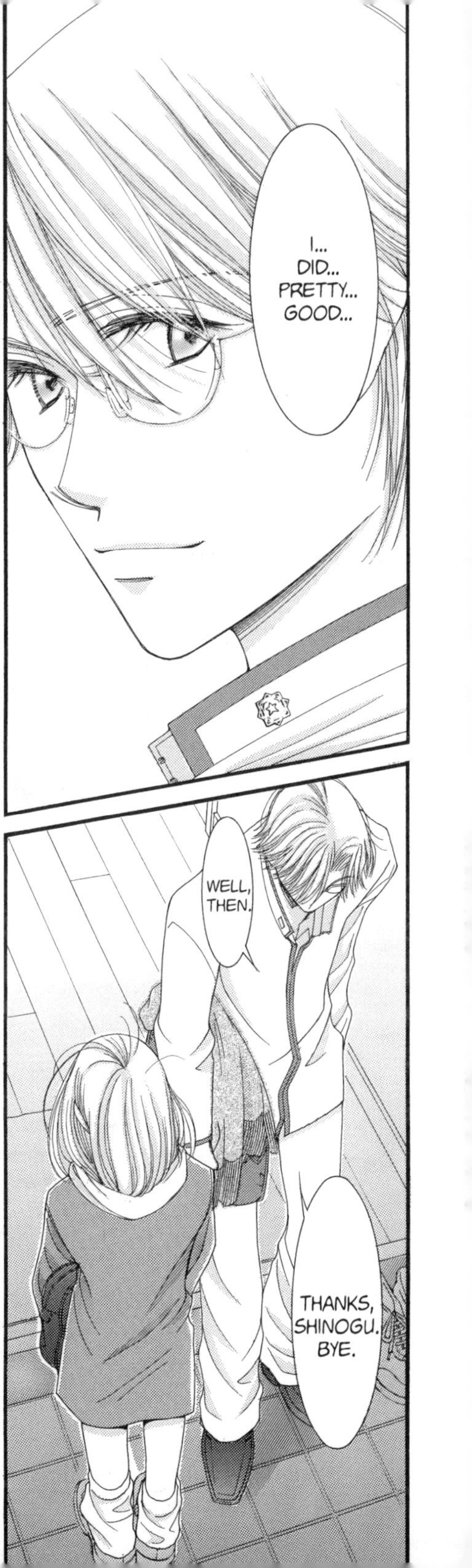

I... DID... PRETTY... GOOD...

WELL, THEN.

THANKS, SHINOGU. BYE.

murmur

...DON'T FORGET.

WE HAD A DEAL.

hotgimmick

Wait a minute! Should I be feeling relieved...?

Chapter 26
Part 1

HMM. AFTER YOUR LAST SEMESTER FINALS, YOU WERE 99th OUT OF 136...

AND NOW, AFTER YOUR FINALS, YOU'RE 64th. THAT'S...

UP 35 PLACES. I WIN!

HA!

HEH HEH HEH HEH HEH HEH
NOW YOU GOTTA DELIVER! ONE DAY OF YOUR VACATION...
INCLUDING THE WHOLE NIGHT!!
SHHHH!!
KEEP YOUR VOICE DOWN!
P... PLUS...
I... UMM...
I CAN'T... SPEND THE NIGHT OUT.
MY DAD'LL BE HOME FOR THE HOLIDAYS, AND...
WELL, MY MOM'S PRETTY STRICT ABOUT STUFF LIKE THAT TOO, PLUS, UMM...
WHAT?!
WHO GOT YOU TO 64th PLACE?!
YOU... DID...
THAT'S RIGHT, AND DON'T FORGET IT! A DEAL IS A DEAL!
GRAB

SO ...
MY FAMILY ALWAYS GETS TOGETHER AT MY GRANDPARENTS' FOR CHRISTMAS EVERY YEAR, SO THAT'S OUT.
THEN, FROM THE 26th THROUGH THE 30th I'M STUCK IN A HOTEL FOR AN INTENSIVE GROUP TUTORIAL, SO THOSE DAYS ARE OUT.
THAT BEING THE CASE, LET'S SET THE DATE.
...WHICH LEAVES NEW YEAR'S EVE! I'LL GET OUT OF THE HOUSE SOMEHOW.
YOU TOO, GOT THAT? COME UP WITH SOME STORY!
ARBITRARY DECISION

If that's how it works...
It's exactly the same as being his slave...
HEFF
What's the point of being his girlfriend (in training) if he never listens to me at all?
NOT ANOTHER BIG SIGH, HATSUMI. DON'T TELL ME YOU'RE DEPRESSED ...
... BECAUSE YOU DON'T HAVE A BOYFRIEND AND HAVE TO SPEND CHRISTMAS AT HOME AGAIN THIS YEAR?
TEE HEE HEE
COME ON! YOU'RE ONLY IN HIGH SCHOOL. YOU'RE TOO YOUNG FOR THAT.
LOOK AT SHINOGU... HE SAID HE'S GOING TO BE WORKING OVER BOTH CHRISTMAS AND THE NEW YEAR AGAIN.
AND HE'S ALWAYS BEEN SO POPULAR, TOO...I WONDER IF HE'S A LATE BLOOMER.
...AND THEN THERE'S ...
BAM!
HEY. HEY! CHECK ME OUT!

SEXY?!
KYEEEEE!
AKANE! WHAT ARE YOU WEARING! YOU LOOK LIKE A TROLLOP!
GYARGH
I'M GOING TO TWO CHRISTMAS PARTIES TONIGHT, BACK-TO-BACK!
Forced to change outfits
I'M SO SURE -- WHAT THE HELL'S A TROLLOP, ANYWAY?
WELL, THAT WAS GOING TOO FAR.
OH, HEY. THAT RE-MINDS ME.
BEEN MEANING TO ASK YOU FOR A WHILE.
HAVE YOU ALREADY **DONE IT** WITH RYOKI?

Voiceless shriek
UMM... WHAT? WHY'S IT SUCH A BIG DEAL?
JUST GO AHEAD AND DO IT.
I ALWAYS WANNA DO IT RIGHT OFF, IF IT'S A GUY I'M REALLY INTO.
HEY, HA-TSUMI...
IS IT REALLY FOR REAL THAT YOU AREN'T IN LOVE WITH RYOKI?
I MEAN, HE'S SOOO NICE TO YOU.
NICE?!
THAT GUY AND THE WORD "NICE" HAVE NOTHING IN COMMON!
OH, COME ON. HE'S ALWAYS TALKING TO YOU AND DOING STUFF WITH YOU AND EVERYTHING.
HE DOESN'T EVEN ***LOOK*** AT GIRLS HE DOESN'T CARE ABOUT.
(Speaking from experience)
YOU MUST BE SUPER SPECIAL TO HIM, HATSUMI.

DA-DOOM
THAT...
...ISN'T... I'M NOT...
Special? Come on. As if...
BUB
UB
And he is not at ALL (well, hardly) nice to me.
He says mean things to me all the time.
And orders me around. And...
OMI... GOD!
Don!

IT'S HERE! JUST LIKE EVERY YEAR! THE STRETCH LIMO...
WHUMP!
LIKE EVERY YEAR...? WHAT'RE YOU TALKING AB--
OH, EXCUSE ME.
DON'T JUST STAND THERE.
YOU'RE IN MY WAY.

WOW! ♡
OMIGOD, IT'S RYOKI-KUN! ARE YOU GOING TO YOUR FAMILY'S BIG CHRISTMAS PARTY? ♡♡
YOU LOOK SO GOOD ALL DRESSED UP LIKE THAT! LIKE A PRINCE OR SOMETHING!
I KNOW.
Like every year...? I never saw this before...
I'M GOING TO A COUPLE CHRISTMAS PARTIES TOO!
PWIK
PARTIES ...?
YOU TOO?
HUH? NO.
I'M STAYING HOME WITH HIKARU...
WHO'S THAT?!
MY BROTHER! MY BABY BROTHER!

...
OH... YEAH.
GOOD.
VERY GOOD. YOU'RE STAYING HOME. I LIKE THAT.
Oh my god.
Some-thing's wrong with me these days.
STAY AT HOME EVERY DAY, TILL THE 30th.
THAT'S AN ORDER.
When he comes close, all dressed up like that...
I don't know why, but my heart starts pounding...
...really hard.
...HEY, YOU LISTENING TO ME?
HEY!
LISTEN TO ME WHEN I'M TALKING TO YOU!
AIRHEAD !!
BONK
!

MASTER RYOKI! YOU SHOULD NOT TREAT A GIRL LIKE THAT.
I'M SO SORRY, MISS NARITA.
AND PLEASE BE SEATED IN THE CAR NOW, MASTER RYOKI.
YOUR MOTHER IS WAITING FOR YOU.
...THAT MY MOM'S? FOR TONIGHT?
YES. I WILL BE ACCOMPANYING YOU TO HELP HER GET DRESSED.
...FER CHRISSAKE... HERE, GIVE IT...
OH.
NO, NO. I CAN CARRY IT. REALLY...
COME ON, GIVE IT.
YOU CAN BE KIND OF A KLUTZ SOMETIMES, MARIKO-SAN.
OH! THAT WAS UNKIND, MASTER RYOKI.

BAM!
GOSH, THEY MUST BE REALLY RICH.
YOU DIDN'T KNOW, HATSUMI? THEY DO THIS EVERY YEAR. ♡
HIS GRAND-PARENTS THROW THIS BIG BASH AT A FANCY HOTEL -- I HEARD MRS. HONDA TALKING ABOUT IT.
LIKE MOVIE STARS! ♡
SO COOL!
YOU'RE SOOO LUCKY, HATSUMI, HAVING SOMEONE LIKE THAT IN LOVE WITH YOU!
HEY, WHEN RYOKI GETS BACK, THE TWO OF YOU SHOULD TAKE OFF AND...
WE'RE NOT GOING ANYWHERE. AND HE ISN'T...IN LOVE WITH ME.
HE JUST THINKS OF ME AS SOME KIND OF SERVANT WHO'LL DO WHATEVER HE SAYS.
I'm not special to him.
Not at all.

That's why...
I can't spend the night with him. Or be his girlfriend-in-training.
I can't do it.
This time, for sure, I'm gonna tell him. Say it real clear.
I'm not spending the night with him.

TMP
YOU MAY GO NOW, HAYASHI.
TMP
THE DAY AFTER TOMORROW, THEN. GOOD NIGHT.
TMP
RYOKI-KUN.
...
...SORRY, MOTHER.
HISS
RYOKI-KUN.
RUSTLE
PLEASE GO HOME WITHOUT ME. I NEED TO GO BUY SOMETHING.
OH... WELL, PLEASE BE CAREFUL, RYOKI DEAR. IT'S LATE.
RUSTLE

HEY, JUNIOR. THIS IS PERFECT.
I WANTED TO TALK TO YOU ABOUT SOME-THING.
SO... NEW YEAR'S EVE. THE 31st. I WANT YOU...
...TO TELL YOUR FOLKS YOU'RE GOING OUT WITH US AND...
THAT AND...
EXCUSE ME!
CAN I ASK YOU SOMETHING FIRST, RYOKI-KUN? QUESTION!
I DON'T KNOW ABOUT "JUNIOR"
...UM, WHAT'S YOUR RELATIONSHIP WITH YOUR MAID?
HUH?
WHAT DO YOU MEAN?
SHE'S OUR MAID. I DON'T GET...
SO, HOW ABOUT MAKING THAT REAL CLEAR TO HATSUMI?!
IT'S MAKING HER REALLY INSECURE.

?
HA-TSUMI'S, LIKE ...
INSECURE? ABOUT WHAT?
...THE TYPE WHO NEEDS TO HAMMER THE HECK OUT OF THE BRIDGE. YOU KNOW, THAT SAYING ABOUT POUNDING A STONE BRIDGE BEFORE YOU CROSS IT?
Image in Ryoki's brain
klonk
klonk
klonk
klonk
SHE NEEDS TO BE REALLY, REALLY SURE ABOUT SOMETHING BEFORE SHE'LL TRUST IT.
I STILL DON'T GET IT...
SET HER STRAIGHT...
...OR YOU'RE NEVER GOING TO GET TO DO IT.
YOU WANT TO SLEEP WITH HER, DON'T YOU?
...THAT'S NONE OF YOUR BUSINESS ...
How'd you know?
LOOK, I'M GOING TO HELP YOU OUT.

IN RETURN FOR WHICH... COULD...
COULD ...
COULD YOU TELL ME WHAT KIND OF GIRL SUBARU LIKES?...YOU KNOW, HIS TYPE...
OR IF...THERE'S SOMEONE HE LIKES... AND STUFF...
...
YOU...
SO!
TO HELP YOU OUT!
WHAT REALLY WORKS WITH HATSUMI, WAY BETTER THAN ORDERING HER AROUND OR YELLING AT HER...
IS JUST SAYING PLEASE. SHE'S A TOTAL PUSHOVER.
TRY BEGGING HER, LIKE WITH TEARS IN YOUR EYES. THAT'S THE WAY TO GO WITH HATSUMI.
PFF!
...GIMME A BREAK.
AS IF I'D EVER DO THAT. TO HER? COME ON.
...WELL, DO WHAT YOU WANT.

TOO BAD, THOUGH. I KNOW SHE'D DO WHATEVER YOU WANTED IF YOU JUST ASKED HER REAL NICE!
I'm so irritated.
Don't really know why.
...I DON'T WANT THIS. I'LL HAVE IT LATER...
THE CHRISTMAS CAKE?
THAT ISN'T LIKE YOU, HATSUMI. WHAT A WASTE...
I'LL EAT IT! LET ME HAVE IT!

OH, HATSUMI. YOU'LL BE HOME FOR NEW YEAR'S, WON'T YOU?
YOUR FATHER'S COMING HOME LATE ON THE 31st, SO MAKE SURE YOU'RE HERE ON NEW YEAR'S EVE.
WE'RE TALKING ABOUT COMBINING HATSUMODE WITH A VISIT TO SHINOGU'S NEW PLACE ON THE FIRST.
NEW YEAR'S EVE! I'LL GET OUT OF THE HOUSE SOMEHOW.
YOU TOO, GOT THAT?
...OKAY.
KA-CHAK!
I'LL BE HERE...
WAIT!
SORRY, MOM! ME AND HATSUMI HAVE TO PASS ON THAT.
THE WHOLE GANG FROM THE COMPLEX IS GOING TO FUKAHARA SHRINE FOR HATSUMODE, ON NEW YEAR'S EVE! WE'LL BE OUT ALL NIGHT!
UM... AKANE? WHAT ARE YOU...
JUST LEAVE THIS TO ME, OKAY?

DON'T WORRY! WE'LL MAKE SURE YOU AND YOUR HONEY-BOY RYOKI GET TO GO OFF ALONE.
PLEEZE, MOM? PLEASE PLEASE PLEASE?
WE ALL WANNA GO TO THE SHRINE TOGETHER. PROMISE TO BE BACK BY NOON THE NEXT DAY, OKAAAY?
I DON'T KNOW... WOULD IT BE SAFE FOR YOU TO BE OUT ALL NIGHT? YOU'RE JUST TEEN-AGERS.
WE'LL BE FINE, MOM. IT'S TOTALLY RIGHT IN THE NEIGHBOR-HOOD! PLUS ASAHI WILL BE THERE, TOO.
PLEEEZE! MOOOM!
WE'RE GIVING YOU A ROCK-SOLID ALIBI, HATSUMI!
How on earth...
25
...did that happen?!
26
I mean... I mean... How...
27
28
29
30

...did this happen?
OMIGOD! LOOK AT THIS.
HUB
NOBODY COMES HERE THE REST OF THE YEAR...
BUB

HA HA HA
WHAT AN HONOR TO HAVE SIR RYOKI TACHIBANA JOIN US!
Gotta tell him.
REMEMBER WE USED TO PLAY HERE A LOT WHEN WE WERE KIDS?
WE HAD SO MUCH FUN!
HEY, BUT THIS MIGHT BE THE FIRST TIME WE'RE HERE WITH RYOKI.
...OH YEAH.
That there's no way I'm spending the night with him.
But...
FLASH
OH, HEY, ASAHI-CHAN. QUICK, OVER HERE! COME ON!
AKANE! I DON'T THINK HATSUMI HEARD...
Ryoki hasn't said a word to me tonight.
Maybe he wasn't serious about that, after all.
Maybe he was just...
...making fun of...

DON'T BE SO NERVOUS.
JUST ACT NORMAL. REAL NATURAL.
BUT, RYOKI...! PEOPLE FROM THE COMPLEX WILL BE HERE.
SO JUST ACT NORMAL. IT'S SO CROWDED THEY WON'T NOTICE!
FIDGET FIDGET FIDGET
MY! IF IT ISN'T RYOKI-KUN!!
GOOD EVENING!
YOICKS!!

ARE YOU ALL DOING HATSUMODE HERE TOGETHER? IT IS LATE AT NIGHT, SO BE CAREFUL, ALL RIGHT?
IS MRS. TACHIBANA ALSO...OH NO, OF COURSE NOT. SHE DOESN'T COME TO SUCH A SMALL SHRINE FOR HATSUMODE.
MY PARENTS ARE SEEING IN THE NEW YEAR WITH MY FATHER'S FAMILY. AS ALWAYS.
I...HAVE TO STUDY, SO I STAYED HOME BY MYSELF.
GOODNESS!
DID YOU HEAR THAT, MASAKAZU? YOU LEARN TO BE MORE LIKE RYOKI-KUN!!
SO STUDIOUS!
WHUMP
HAVE A HAPPY NEW YEAR! AND BE CAREFUL!
GIVE MY BEST REGARDS TO YOUR MOTHER, RYOKI-KUN!
THANK YOU, MRS. HONDA, I'LL DO THAT...
HEE HEE
SEE? SHE DIDN'T NOTICE.
PIECE OF CAKE! THANK YOU, NEW YEAR HORDES!
RYOKIIIII...
GOD, I WISH IT WAS ALWAYS THIS CROWDED!

?
BLUSH
Gosh. I never saw him...
He can be really cute some-times.
...smile like that before.
WE'RE GOING TO THE STATION, GETTING ON THE TRAIN, AND SPENDING THE NIGHT TOGETHER, WHAT ELSE?!
WHAD-DAYA MEAN, "HUH?"
YANK
GREAT, SHE SAW US. NOW YOU CAN COVER FOR US, SUBARU.
COME ON, WE'RE OUTTA HERE.
...HUH?

WHA... WHOA, WHOA, WHOA, WHOA!
NO!
I CAN'T DO THIS AFTER ALL.
I CAN'T TELL MY PARENTS I SPENT THE NIGHT WITH YOU, PLUS I HAVEN'T PACKED ANYTHING OR ANYTHING...
I CAN'T GO.
...BUT WE HAD A DEAL...
AND YOU DON'T HAVE TO TELL YOUR PARENTS. GET JUNIOR TO COVER FOR YOU.
I DON'T WANT TO GO!

I need to talk about this first.
WHAT?
HUH?
FLUSTER
FLUSTER
YOU'RE GOING WHERE?
I need to take it real slow.
Real slow. Otherwise...
I...
WHAT REALLY WORKS WITH HATSUMI... IS JUST SAYING PLEASE. SHE'S A TOTAL PUSHOVER.
HMPH!
YOU KIDDING ME?!!
...GIMME A BREAK.

WE HAD A GODDAMN AGREEMENT! WHAT THE HELL IS WITH YOU...
RYO! UH... HEY, RYO!
DRRR
DRRRR
OH...
...THAT MINE?
YEAH. UH... OH.
BIP
MARIKO-SAN.
...WHAT? SO WAIT A MINUTE, YOU MEAN...
OKAY, STAY RIGHT THERE. I'LL BE THERE IN A SEC.

JUST DON'T MOVE. WAIT FOR ME, OKAY?
YEAH. BYE...
BIP!
HUH? WHERE YOU GOING, RYO?
EMER-GENCY.
HATSUMI, WAIT FOR ME AT THE BACK OF THE SHRINE.
IF I'M NOT BACK IN HALF AN HOUR, GO HOME AND PACK. I'LL COME GET YOU.
LIVE
YOU GOT THAT, BONEHEAD ?!
HEY...
RYO! HEY...
See?

UH... HATSUMI? UMM...
I DON'T REALLY GET WHAT'S GOING ON HERE...
I knew it.
I told you, Akane.
I told you I'm not special to him. Not the least bit.
He doesn't care how I feel. He doesn't listen to me.
But if Mariko-san calls him, he'll rush off in two seconds.
UH... WELL...HOW ABOUT WE LOOK FOR THE OTHERS AND...
SORRY... I'M GOING HOME.
WHAT? BUT... HANG ON, HATSUMI.
I THOUGHT RYO SAID TO WAIT FOR HIM...

I don't care.
Should've known. That being his girlfriend-in-training wouldn't work out.
Oh well.
At least this way I don't have to go.
Yeah, it worked out fine. Don't have to spend the night with him.
Don't have to worry about stuff. So, great! This is just fine!

I HATE HIM.
I REALLY DO.

hotgimmick

PART 2
OF CHAPTER 26
PRESENTS
RYOKI'S POINT
OF VIEW...

←

Chapter
26
Part 2

YOU AREN'T SERIOUS, DARLING?
ABOUT STAYING HERE ALONE OVER THE NEW YEAR?
I AM, MOTHER. I'M **VERY** SERIOUS.
WELL... ALL RIGHT.
DO AS YOU WISH, RYOKI DEAR.
JUST TELL THE OLD BAG I WANT TO CONCENTRATE ON MY STUDIES OR SOMETHING LIKE THAT...
SHE ALWAYS FALLS FOR IT. IT'S A TOTAL CINCH.
THERE.

IF FOR SOME REASON WE DON'T (WELL, I'M MAKING SURE WE DO, DAMMIT)...
TELL THE TRUTH, THOUGH...
SINCE YOU'RE NOT COMING WITH US FOR THE NEW YEAR, DARLING...
BE SURE TO SPEND A LOT OF TIME WITH YOUR GRAND-PARENTS AT TONIGHT'S CHRISTMAS PARTY.
JUST BEING ALONE WITH HATSUMI...
TWO MORE DAYS...
THE TWO OF US...
THIS TIME, FOR SURE...
WE'RE DOING IT.

... AND JUST HOLDING HER CLOSE TO ME ...
... WOULD BE PRETTY GREAT, IS WHAT I WAS THINKING ...
HUFF
BUT THAT DOPE (GRRR) ...
MARIKO-SAN!
OH, MY...
YOU DIDN'T HAVE TO RUN ALL THE WAY...
AFTER WHAT YOU JUST TOLD ME?
THAT WE WOULDN'T BE ABLE TO GET IN? WHAT THE HELL... MARIKO-SAN?
WELL, MASTER RYOKI, I DECIDED TO ASK YOUR MOTHER ABOUT IT, JUST IN CASE.
AND APPARENTLY, FOR SECURITY REASONS... THEY'VE CHANGED THE LOCKS. SO THE KEY YOU HAD WOULD NOT HAVE WORKED.
HOWEVER, I WAS ABLE TO "BORROW" THE SPARE KEY.
THANKS, MARIKO-SAN...
YOU'VE REALLY SAVED MY DAY HERE.
YOU'RE VERY WELCOME, MASTER RYOKI.
PHEW

OF ALL OUR VACATION PLACES...
...IT'S MY FAVORITE.
AND THERE, WE WON'T RUN INTO ANYBODY FROM THE COMPLEX, SO...
...THAT CAUTIOUS IDIOT WILL FINALLY BE ABLE TO RELAX AND...
LET'S SKIP THE "IN TRAINING" THING, AFTER ALL...
LET ME BE YOUR GIRL-FRIEND FOR REAL.
WELL THEN, MASTER RYOKI...
I BETTER BE GETTING BACK TO YOUR GRAND-PARENTS' HOUSE.
OH, YEAH. RIGHT.
TEE HEE
...WHAT?
IT'S JUST THAT...
THINGS ARE TURNING OUT EXACTLY THE WAY I SAID THEY WOULD. DO YOU RE-MEMBER?

GIRLS ARE SO DARN STUPID.
WHO NEEDS THEM?
ALL THEY'RE GOOD FOR IS SEX. THEY'RE JUST BODIES, BASICALLY.
SMAK!
IF THAT IS YOUR ATTITUDE, MASTER RYOKI...
YOU ARE GOING TO RUN INTO A LOT OF DIFFICULTIES WHEN YOU FINALLY MEET SOMEONE SPECIAL.
...WHO SAYS HATSUMI...
...IS SO SPECIAL TO ME, ANYWAY?
MM-HMM.
I THINK YOU SHOULD HURRY OFF NOW, MASTER RYOKI.

THE PROBLEM IS...
I DON'T WANT TO GO!
FIVE MINUTES TO THE SHRINE...
IF WE GO STRAIGHT TO THE STATION, WE'LL MAKE THE TRAIN.
JEEZ, THOUGH, THAT BONE-HEAD.
PULLING THIS CRAP ON ME AFTER ALL I WENT THROUGH TO MAKE THIS HAPPEN, FER CHRISSAKE.
DING!
TRY BEGGING HER, LIKE WITH TEARS IN YOUR EYES.
GIMME A GODDAMN BREAK! YOU KIDDING ME? WHY THE HELL SHOULD I HAVE TO...

HEY!
WHAT THE HELL ARE YOU DOING, HEADING HOME ALREADY?
I TOLD YOU TO WAIT FOR ME AT THE BACK OF THE SHRINE...

...
HEY... WHAT HAP-PENED?
IS SOMETHING THE MATTER?
NO... IT'S NOTHING. OKAY?!
AND WHAT ABOUT... YOU, RYOKI...? WHY...
...ARE YOU HERE...?
NOTHING'S THE MATTER?
SO WHY'RE YOU CRYING?
I AM NOT CRYING!
WELL, BYE THEN. GOOD NIGHT.
HAVE A HAPPY NEW YEAR.
HELLO?!
DON'T JERK ME AROUND! WHAT'S THE MATTER WITH YOU?
BUT... I TOLD YOU I'M NOT GOING.
WE HAD A DEAL!
BUT...
I WAS TRYING...
...TO...

...TO EXPLAIN...
GUSH
TO TELL YOU HOW I FEEL...
HUH ?!
BUT YOU JUST...

JUST DITCHED ME... AND WENT OFF...
THIS WAS ABOUT ME ?!
LIKE, LIKE...ALWAYS... YOU NEVER, EVER...LISTEN TO ME...
TO WHAT I HAVE TO SAY...
HIC
YOU, YOU SAID... I COULD JUST BE... "IN TRAINING" BUT...
HIC
...THEN ALL YOU... WANT...IS TO SLEEP WITH ME RIGHT AWAY...AND THEN...
WHEN I SAY NO, YOU... YOU SAY IT'S... AN ORDER, SO...
HIC
SHE...
...HATES THE THOUGHT OF GOING SO MUCH IT'S MAKING HER CRY?
IT ISN'T ANY DIFFERENT FROM BEFORE. YOU STILL TREAT ME LIKE YOUR SLAVE. AND YOU HIT ME AND SAY MEAN THINGS TO ME...
HIC
BUT WITH MARIKO-SAN, YOU'RE ALWAYS REALLY NICE...
HIC
HUH?!
WHY DOES MARIKO-SAN COME INTO THIS?
HIC
HIC
I GIVE UP. I JUST DON'T UNDER-STAND.

BUT...
STILL...
ARGH.
DAMMIT... I CAN'T HELP IT.

SHE'S
JUST
TOO
DAMN
CUTE.

GRR
OKAY, FINE.
HEY...
I'LL DO IT. IF THAT'S WHAT IT TAKES, I'LL DO IT.
RYOKI... PEOPLE WILL...
1
"BEG HER WITH TEARS IN YOUR EYES."
...HA-TSUMI.
2
"SAY PLEASE."
YOU DON'T WANT TO GO?
YOU HATE BEING WITH ME SO MUCH?
HUH ...?
BECAUSE I WANT YOU TO COME.
I REALLY, REALLY...
...WANT YOU TO COME WITH ME.
Thinks he's saying please.

I REALLY DO.
SO MUCH...

...I...
OKAY... I'LL... GO...
SO... STOP STARING AT ME...UP CLOSE LIKE THAT...
IF IT'S...JUST FOR A WHILE...
I'LL GO...
THAT WAS EASY. THAT WAS SO EASY!

hotgimmick

When he was thinking how easy it was.
(Surface expression)
How Ryoki looked to Hatsumi...

By the way, Ryoki's tuxedo look in Chapter 26 was referred to as "mafia don-chic" by the staff... while readers writing to Betsucomi's "Gimmick Cafe" thought he looked like a male escort...

Chapter 27

hotgimmick

December 31.
A little after
11:30 p.m.

HEY, IT'S ASAHI!
OH HI, YOU GUYS!
HOW YOU DOIN'? OMIGOD, I CAN'T BELIEVE YOU'RE ALL HERE!
HEY, SHE'S CUTE!
UM, ASAHI?
I'M GONNA GO LOOK FOR HATSUMI AND THE OTHERS, OKAY? I'LL SEE YOU LATER.
OH, OKAY.
SHE'S GOING?
WHAAT?
SORRY, AKANE! I'LL MEET UP WITH YOU GUYS LATER.
HEE HEE! ACTUALLY, HATSUMI AND RYOKI...
OUGHT TO HAVE SNEAKED OFF BY NOW! ♡
AT LEAST I HOPE THEY DID...
...OH. HEY...!

LIVE
SONIC LAB
SOOBAROO! WHAT'S UP?
OH!
AKANE! RYO AND HATSUMI... THEY BOTH WENT OFF SOME-WHERE!
WHAT ARE WE SUPPOSED TO DO? THEY JUST TOOK OFF...

THEY DID?
THAT'S GREAT! DON'T WORRY ABOUT THEM. THEY JUST... HAD A DATE, THAT'S ALL. ♡
...WHAT ...?
THE ONLY REASON WE ALL CAME OUT TOGETHER WAS TO GIVE THEM AN ALIBI. OOH, I BET THEY'RE ALL KISSY-KISSY BY NOW! ♡
IF YOU'RE WORRIED, WE CAN TRY CALLING RYOKI'S CELL...
KI...
KISSY... KISSY...?
LIVE
OH... YEAH... SO THAT'S... WHAT IT WAS...
OKAY... I GET IT... A DATE, HUH...? GREAT...
GUESS THEY'RE ALL RIGHT THEN... IF THEY'RE TOGETH-ER...
ALL KISSY-KISSY... AND EVERY-THING...
STRUGGLING TO LOOK CALM
...JUST LIKE I THOUGHT. YOU DO HAVE A CRUSH ON HATSUMI, DON'T YOU?
I...

PFUT
...IT'S OKAY. I TOTALLY KNOW.
YOU DON'T LIKE ME. IT'S AS SIMPLE AS THAT.
LIVE
THAT'S WHY YOU'RE ALWAYS IGNORING ME...
I KNEW IT. DARN...
I... NO, UH...
DON'T... LIKE YOU? THAT'S --
YO! HEY GUYS, IT'S AKANE!
SWARM
SWARM
YOU WERE HERE?! JEEZ, GIRL. WHY DIDN'T YOU CALL US?
HEY, HANG OUT WITH US TONIGHT!
YEAH, WE'RE GOING OVER TO YAMADA'S LATER. PARTY!
...
shut out

SORRY, GUYS!
NOT TONIGHT. NEXT TIME, OKAY?
I'M WITH SOME-ONE!
WHAAA?
KRUNCH
NO WAY, REALLY?!
YEAH, SO...
COME ON...
NO WAAAY
IS THAT FOR REAL?
HAVE A HAPPY NEW YEAR, YOU GUYS!

I COULDN'T JUST LEAVE YOU ALL ALONE, COULD I!?
CUZ, WELL, YOU LOOKED KINDA LONELY AND STUFF.
...I MEAN ...
BEING WITH A GIRL YOU DON'T LIKE... IS STILL BETTER THAN BEING ALONE, RIGHT?
IT'S NO FUN DOING HATSUMODE BY YOUR-SELF...
I...
I DO LIKE YOU!
UH... IT'S...

JUST...
YOU SCARE ME.
OH YEAH?! WELL, EXCUSE ME ALL TO HELL!
KA-BOOM
SORRY I'M NOT ALL NAMBY-PAMBY LIKE HATSUMI, OKAY?!
GYAAGH!
...AND FOR NOT BEING LIKE GUNDAM, EITHER.
HUH
?
RYOKI TOLD ME! HE SAID...
"ALL I KNOW IS HE'S CRAZY ABOUT GUNDAM... SO, I GUESS HIS TYPE WOULD BE...A GIRL LIKE GUNDAM?"
Something like this?
I'M NOT REALLY UP ON THAT STUFF...IS GUNDAM A FEMALE ROBOT OR SOMETHING?
CREST-FALLEN
You've got me all wrong... (sob)
No, Ryo...
...NO, BUT...
SEE, WHAT I DON'T GET...
YOU WERE ALWAYS CALLING ME A DWEEB AND STUFF, CUZ I'M INTO GUNDAM AND SHONEN JUMP...
SO...HOW COME... YOU SUDDENLY SAY...
YOU... LOVE ME...?
KUCH

I MEAN, I DIDN'T CHANGE OR ANYTHING...
I'M STILL...A DWEEB...
I THOUGHT YOU WERE TEASING ME OR...
YOU ARE SO STUPID.
THAT'S JUST HOW IT IS. IT JUST HAPPENS, OKAY?
LOVE JUST HITS YOU LIKE THAT SOMETIMES.
I CAN'T BELIEVE HOW CLUELESS YOU ARE.

I WASN'T TEASING YOU.
LOOK, I'M GOING TO SAY IT AGAIN, OKAY?
I LOVE YOU, SUBARU.
I WANT YOU TO BE MY BOYFRIEND.
STIR
FIVE!
WHAT'S GOING ON?!
FOUR!
OH...
LIVE

hotgimmick

The same day, just a little after 11:00 p.m.
IT'S ABOUT TWO MORE STOPS.
Argh.
THERE SHOULD BE A CAR WAITING FOR US OUTSIDE THE STATION, SO DON'T SCREW AROUND.
I don't believe this.
I SAID "VACATION HOME," BUT ACTUALLY IT'S JUST A SUITE IN A HOTEL, SO IT'S NOT THAT BIG OR ANY-THING.
I left without saying any-thing to Mom.
And Dad... should be coming home right around now...
WHAT?! HATSUMI AND AKANE ARE OUT?!
AT THIS HOUR?!
I WANT THEM HOME!!
UNCHAPER-ONED?! GET AKANE ON HER CELL PHONE THIS INSTANT!
No no no no no no. I don't care. I'm not listening to Dad, anyway!

URGH
SO PLEASE, HATSUMI... DON'T EVEN THINK ABOUT GOING OUT WITH RYOKI, OKAY?
I NEVER WANT TO GO THROUGH THAT AGAIN...
Stab
Stab
URGH
WHAT? HATSUMI AND AKANE ARE OUT ...?
I WAS HOPING I'D SEE THEM AT NEW YEAR'S AT LEAST...
WHAT A BUMMER...
Shinogu...
There's no way I could tell Shinogu, either, that I'm going out with Ryo...
SHWOOOO
LAW OF THE IRON FIST
I SAID, LISTEN TO ME...
HEY! I'M TALKING TO YOU. FER CHRISSAKE!
...WELL.
COME THIS FAR, AND EVEN YOU WON'T BE ABLE TO GET AWAY THIS TIME.

HA HA HA HA HA
YOU ARE SOOO SIMPLE!
HA HA HA HA HA
ALL I HAVE TO DO IS PRETEND TO BEG A LITTLE, AND YOU SAY YES.
HA HA HA HA HA
WHAT A CINCH THAT WAS! TOTAL PIECE OF CAKE!
PRE... TEND... TO BEG...?
I REALLY, REALLY WANT YOU TO COME WITH ME...
THOUGH, IF YOU ASK ME...
IT'S THE LEAST YOU DESERVE FOR TRYING TO CALL OFF OUR DEAL AT THE LAST MINUTE.
MORON!
flash

He...
fweeee
... tricked me...
SHWUUMP
WAAAARGH ...
I AM SOOOOO STUUUPIIID ...
HEY! STAND UP! GET OVER HERE, THE CAR'S WAITING.
JEEZ, I'M TIRED.
CAN'T WAIT TO TAKE A NICE HOT BATH AND GO TO BED...
YULP!
GO...

...
TO
BED
?!

...MAN, I NEVER EXPECTED TO SPEND NEW YEAR'S EVE WAY THE HELL OUT IN IZU...
DUDE, IT COULD BE A HELL OF A LOT WORSE!
THE PAY'S REAL GOOD, AND IT'S JUST ONE NIGHT. I SAY WE GOT REAL LUCKY.
KA-CHAK
C'MON, DUDE, WE'RE GOIN'.

NARITA, C'MON.
...I'M COMING...
I DON'T KNOW ABOUT THIS, THOUGH, KAZAMA...
THIS PLACE IS TOTALLY POSH. WE JUST BLOW IN WITHOUT ANY TRAINING OR ANYTHING...
DON'T SWEAT IT, DUDE, IT'S JUST ONE NIGHT. PLUS WE AIN'T DEALIN' WITH THE GUESTS. Y'ALL JUST RELAX.
BUT HOW THE HELL DID YOU GET US THIS JOB IN THE FIRST PLACE? I MEAN...
Y'ALL DON'T BOTHER YOURSELF ABOUT THAT, DUDE.
OH, HEY! WHAT'S BOTHERIN' ME...DUDE! IS IT TRUE...
THAT GORGEOUS SAKURADA-CHAN ASKED YOU OUT AND Y'ALL TURNED HER DOWN?!
SAKURA...? OH, YEAH...
I JUST DON'T GET IT. HOW COME, DUDE? WOMEN LOVE YA. HOW COME YOU AIN'T GOT A GIRLFRIEND?
WOPE!
DON'T TELL ME YOU'RE QUEER OR SOMETHIN'?! CUZ I AIN'T, OKAY? CAN'T HELP YOU OUT THERE!
Aiee!
Chill, chill.

OH... I GOT IT. IT'S LIKE THIS.
YOU IN LOVE WITH SOMEONE, AIN'T YOU? THERE'S SOME GIRL OUT THERE YOU'RE NUTS ABOUT, AND...
PHWEEEN
YOU TWO! YOU THE PART-TIMERS?
NO CHATTING WHILE ON DUTY.
COME OVER HERE AND GET YOUR INSTRUCTIONS FROM THE CHIEF.
YESSIR!
SORRY!
SORRY!
HEY. DUDE. DUDE!
I'M TALKIN' TO YA!
NO CHAT-TING WHILE ON DUTY!
WELL, WHAT ABOUT YOU? YOU'RE SINGLE...
OH, ME?
I'M LOOKIN' FOR THE GIRL OF MY DREAMS, MYSELF!
AND WHAT DREAMS I GOT!
NO CHATTING WHILE ON DUTY!

WELL... GUESS THE YEAR'S ALMOST OVER...
...
WONDER WHAT SHE'S DOING RIGHT NOW.
HATSUMI ...
IF THAT IS ALL, MASTER TACHIBANA...
I'LL BE LEAVING YOU NOW.
THANK YOU.

OH... MY... GOD...
No! No no no no! This is no time for gawping!
GULP
Right now I need to worry about...

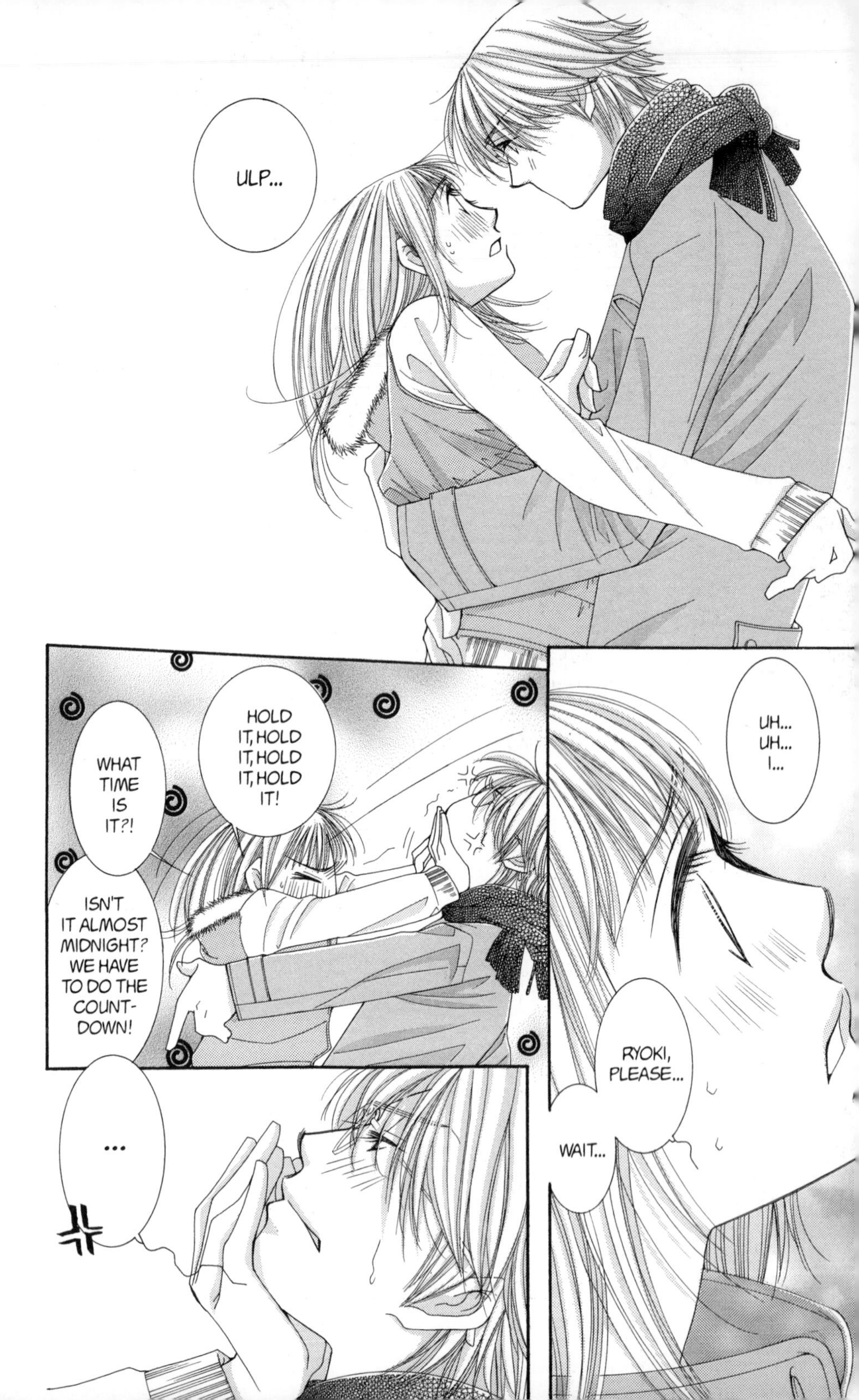
ULP...
UH... UH... I...
RYOKI, PLEASE...
WAIT...
HOLD IT, HOLD IT, HOLD IT, HOLD IT!
WHAT TIME IS IT?!
ISN'T IT ALMOST MIDNIGHT? WE HAVE TO DO THE COUNT-DOWN!
...

FWUMP
TEN MORE MINUTES!
SO, UH... I THINK I'LL GO EXPLORE THE HOTEL A LITTLE, OKAY?
I'LL BE RIGHT BACK! LET ME HAVE THE KEY!
SLAM
...WELL, NO BIG DEAL. THE LAST TRAIN BACK TO TOKYO'S GONE ALREADY...
WHAT'S WITH THE STUPID COUNT-DOWN, ANYWAY? WHO CARES?
Now what? Now what? Now what?
HFFF

POOF!
Oh, come on! You can't say you don't want to sleep with him **NOW**, after coming all the way out here with him.
LITTLE DEMON NARITA
But he tricked me!
ANGEL NARITA

Yeah, sure.
Actually, you were pretty happy to see him coming back to the shrine so soon to meet you. Weren't you?
Ulp! Well, that's ...

THUMP

Plus ...
The reason you're upset about Mariko-san is that you never saw Ryoki being nice to any girl besides you before...
And that came as a shock, didn't it?

In other words...
You're jealous!
Aren't you?

No I'm not...

Well... maybe I... am?

!...
...ER...
ARE YOU ALL RIGHT, MISS? DO YOU FEEL ILL...?
OH, NO. I'M FINE...
YULP!

SHINOGU...
HUH...? HOW COME...?!
WHY'RE ***YOU*** HERE?! I THOUGHT... I MEAN, MOM SAID...
WE'D BE VISITING YOU TOMORROW AT YOUR NEW PLACE!
UH... THIS JOB HERE CAME UP.
ALL OF A SUDDEN. I JUST GOT HERE TODAY.
BUT WHAT'RE ***YOU*** DOING HERE, HATSUMI? YOU STAYING HERE?
URGH!

UH...
YEAH! YEAH, I AM!
Omigod, now what? Gyaaak!
YOU ARE?
BUT THIS IS A PRIVATE RESORT. I THOUGHT IT WAS MEMBERS-ONLY.
Make something up! Make something up!
UH... UMM...A FRIEND OF MINE!
A FRIEND OF MINE'S DAD... IS A MEMBER, AND HE, UH, INVITED A BUNCH OF US TO STAY!
HFF
GULP
WHAT? WHAT?!
NOTHING. I JUST DIDN'T THINK...
...I'D GET TO SEE YOU... UH, ALL THE WAY OUT HERE.
UM, SHI-NOGU?
HOW LONG'S THIS JOB FOR...?
I'LL BE DONE AT NOON TOMOR-ROW.
WANNA MEET UP AND GO HOME TOGETHER?
NO! I MEAN, I CAN'T! CUZ I'M WITH MY FRIENDS...!

NARITA.
WE ALL GOTTA GO TO THE LINEN ROOM.
OH. GOTCHA.
UH, BYE, SHINOGU.
I'LL SEE YOU TOMORROW. GOOD LUCK WITH THE JOB.
HAVE A HAPPY NEW YEAR.
YEAH. YOU TOO, HATSUMI.

HELP!! THIS TOTALLY SUCKS!

GOTTA MAKE SURE HE DOESN'T FIND OUT!

IF SHINOGU FOUND OUT ABOUT RYOKI...

...I'D JUST ABOUT DIE...

WHAT'RE YOU SMILING ABOUT?
OHHH. IT'S THAT GUEST YOU WERE TALKIN' TO, HUH?
SHE TRY TO PICK YOU UP? SHE DID, HUH?
SHE ASK Y'ALL TO COME TO HER ROOM LATER?
NO. COME ON. DIDN'T YOU NOTICE? THAT WAS...
PRIVATE ROOM
MR. NARITA.
YES-SIR!
DELIVER THIS TO GUEST SERVICE, PLEASE.
IT'S A WELCOME BOUQUET FOR THE GUESTS IN SUITE 3006.
YES, SIR...
WOW, THAT'S A FANCY BOU-QUET...
SO HANDLE IT WITH THE UTMOST CARE, IF YOU WILL.
AND MAKE SURE YOU GIVE THEM THIS CARD WITH IT!
YES... SIR...
For Mr. Ryoki Tachibana

RYO...
KI... TACHI...
HEY! WHAT'RE YOU DOIN', YA DOPE?
SO... HER FRIEND ...
...IS RYOKI ...?
Exactly 11:55 p.m.

I'll try explaining to Ryoki...
...that my brother's here.
CHAK

HUH...?
HE'S NOT HERE...?

Where'd he go? I hope he isn't mad at me.
BM
BM
Now what?
I wonder where he went off...

HEY...
RYO... KI...?

RYO... KI...?
HE ISN'T... FOOLING? HE'S ACTUALLY ASLEEP? FOR REAL?
RYOOO-KIIII...!
SSSS
...BONE-HEAD.
MEANIE.
TREMBLE
TREMBLE
PSHHH
ARRO-GANT, BOSSY...
... SELFISH JERK...
FAST ASLEEP
I guess...
He must've been really tired.

Well...
I sure got to see different sides of Ryoki today.
When he's sleeping...
He isn't scary at all.

OH, DAMN...
THE COUNT-DOWN'S STARTED, RYOKI!
FIVE.
I got it.
FOUR.
I just figured out why my heart starts throbbing...
...when I'm with Ryoki.

It's because...
Even though he scares me...
...and I know I really shouldn't...
I can't stop myself...
...from falling in love with him...

So I don't know what to do.

And that...

...makes me feel more and more nervous around him.

TWO!
ONE!

IT WOULD BE NICE...
...IF HE'D BE A LITTLE LESS SCARY THIS YEAR...
0:00 A.M.
HAPPY NEW YEAR!

To be continued

Thank you for buying Hot Gimmick Vol. 6.
My name is Miki Aihara.
Here, just for you graphic novel readers, is extra information that's so hard to put into the actual story.
Read on!

FIRST OF ALL, A THANK YOU AND AN APOLOGY ON BEHALF OF THE AUTHOR... THANK YOU, EVERYBODY, FOR ALL YOUR E-MAILS AND LETTERS! SHE READS EVERY SINGLE ONE.
AND SORRY ABOUT NOT WRITING BACK...SHE REALLY WANTS TO, BUT SHE JUST DOESN'T HAVE A SINGLE SPARE MINUTE RIGHT NOW. HER DEEPEST APOLOGIES.

...BY THE WAY...A LOT OF THE MAIL ASKS ABOUT SHINOGU AND WHY HE HAS SO MANY PART-TIME JOBS.

WHY IS THAT, SHINO-GU?

WELL... IT'S CUZ I WANT TO PAY MY OWN RENT AND LIVING EXPENSES... SO THAT DOESN'T LEAVE ME ANY TIME FOR GOOFING AROUND.

← But this uniform is simply a matter of taste... Mine and my assistant S-chan's!

AND WHAT ABOUT AZUSA? ISN'T HE GOING TO BE IN THE STORY ANYMORE?! A LOT OF READERS WANT TO KNOW, SO LET'S ASK THE GUY HIMSELF.

THAT'S A SECRET!

AND NOW...IT'S BEEN A WHILE SINCE WE INTRODUCED ANY GIMMICK FAMILIES TO YOU... FINALLY, HERE THEY ARE... ←

The Tachibana Family and Someone Who Works For Them

RYOKI (17)

- SECOND-YEAR STUDENT AT THE PRESTIGIOUS PRIVATE KAISEI ACADEMY.
- 177 cm TALL, 61 kg. (BUT STILL GROWING. A LOT TO GO.)
- WAS SICK DURING ENTRANCE EXAMS FOR PRIVATE ELEMENTARY SCHOOLS, SO HE WAS FORCED TO GO TO PUBLIC SCHOOL THROUGH SIXTH GRADE. (MAJOR SOURCE OF SHAME TO MRS. T.) SPENT ALL JUNIOR HIGH VACATIONS ABROAD, SO SPEAKS PERFECT ENGLISH.

NATSUE TACHIBANA

- UNDISPUTED QUEEN OF THE COMPANY HOUSING COMPLEX.
- FORMER BEAUTY WHO WAS ONCE CROWNED MISS KOBE.
- HOBBIES INCLUDE THE TEA CEREMONY, IKEBANA AND HAIKU.
- MARRIAGE TO MR. TACHIBANA WAS ARRANGED BY THEIR PARENTS.

MARIKO TAKATO (23)

- SERVED IN THE TACHIBANA HOUSEHOLD (RYOKI'S GRANDPARENTS) FROM A YOUNG AGE, DUE TO HER PARENTS' WORK SITUATION.
- HAS KNOWN RYOKI SINCE HE WAS IN ELEMENTARY SCHOOL.

THERE'S A LOT MORE TO TELL ABOUT THE TACHIBANAS, BUT LET'S LEAVE IT AT THIS FOR NOW! AND THAT'S ALL THE EXTRA FOR TODAY, FOLKS.

SHUICHIRO TACHIBANA

- AT LAST HE MAKES AN APPEARANCE!
- WENT TO SAME UNIVERSITY AS THE OTHER DADS, BUT A FEW YEARS AHEAD OF THEM.
- MOSTLY STAYS AT A HOTEL NEAR THE COMPANY, SO HARDLY EVER RETURNS TO THE COMPLEX. (UNLIKE HIS WIFE, HAS ABSOLUTELY NO INTEREST IN THE GOINGS-ON THERE.)

Author Notes

Volume 4

About Volume 3's cover... There seemed to be some confusion about the person on the cover, so I wish to apologize. It wasn't Shinogu, but was actually Azusa. I didn't realize that the topic of Azusa's hair hadn't come up until this volume, so I inadvertently drew him with short hair. (If you're saying that you can't tell the difference between the two characters from my drawing, you'd be right... *Sob.*) But it's Azusa. Shinogu is on the cover of this volume. I'm sorry.

Volume 5

We've come to the fifth volume. I'd like to thank everyone who has bought this series. I'm only able to do this because of the efforts of my editor, the entire editorial staff and my super assistants who have come to my rescue. I'm really sorry for all the inconvenience I've caused with my lateness. Thank you so much, everyone.

Volume 6

We've come to the sixth volume—all thanks to my readers who have supported this series so far. As this is my longest series to date, I've been over-thinking things so much that I'm causing trouble for everyone around me. I am so sorry. It's like I'm realizing my own inadequacies. But as far as *Hot Gimmick* goes, there are still things I want to draw, or that I haven't been able to draw yet, so... *(laugh)* Please stick with me though. It'll take some time, but I will do my best.

IN THE NEXT VOLUME
Just when Hatsumi and Ryoki's relationship is *finally* about to take a turn for the better, it seems like all the forces of nature are out to destroy it. With neither family's approval, both their mothers try their best to keep the two apart. And Azusa's search for the truth about his mother's past may reveal more than just an affair between her and Hatsumi's father—the revelations may drive Shinogu to do something that will tear the Narita family apart. Will Shinogu's secret force him to disappear from Hatsumi's life forever? Find out in the next titillating volume of *Hot Gimmick!*
VOLUME 3
Available Now